The Shape of the Past 2

Essays in Scottish Ethnology

ALEXANDER FENTON

Research Director, National Museums of Scotland

A Scottish History and Culture Paperback

JOHN DONALD PUBLISHERS LTD
EDINBURGH

ISBN 0 85976 141 X

Exclusive distribution in the United States of
America and Canada by Humanities Press Inc.,
Atlantic Highlands, NJ 07716, USA.

Tibi

Filmset by Burns & Harris Limited, Dundee
Printed in Great Britain by Bell & Bain Ltd., Glasgow

Acknowledgements

Grateful acknowledgement is made to the editors of the publications in which these essays first appeared, as follows, following the essay numbers:

1. *Národopisný Věstnik Československý* III-IV (1969), 17-51.

2. *A Magyar Mezögazdasági Múzeum Közlemeńyei* 1971-72, 69-75.

3. *In Memoriam António Jorge Dias* Lisbon 1974, 147-186.

4-5. Gailey, A. and Fenton, A. *The Spade in Northern and Atlantic Europe* Belfast 1970, 155-193.

6. *Folk Life* II (1964), 3-26.

I am also grateful to Colin Hendry, F.S.A. Scot, for drawing or re-drawing most of the illustrative diagrams.

Annie Stirling Stronach
1904-1984

Contents

Introduction

This second volume of essays on *The Shape of the Past* draws on material previously published in Czechoslovakia, Hungary and Portugal, as well as in Britain. In some cases re-arrangements have been made, and the opportunity has been taken to include a greatly improved series of diagrams. In particular, the ox-yoke illustrations provide as complete a corpus of early Irish and Scottish finds as has ever appeared in this country. They constitute valuable source-material for archaeologists as well as all others interested in the history of transport and draught.

The last four essays look in considerable detail at the subjects of seaweed manure, turf and peat. These have had a great influence on productivity and on patterns of land-use and settlement. Estate plans can give the general layout of fields and rigs, and may indicate the kinds of crops grown, but in order to get a lively sense of how people operated on the land and how they thought of what they were doing, it is necessary to look closely at topics such as those selected here. However neglected by scholars such mundane subjects have been, nevertheless they help to provide insight into the ways of our ancestors in a way that is scarcely possible otherwise. Concern for getting food is one of the deepest motivations of humanity, singly and in communities. These essays look at how people strove to improve the fertility of the soil that produced for them the bread of life.

It is also of much interest to see how, over the centuries, the use of turf for manure and of peat for fuel (the ashes of which also went back on to the land) has cleared and changed now unimaginable stretches of the countryside. The influence of man on the landscape is nothing new at all.

Alexander Fenton

Part I

Yokes and Oxen

1
Draught Oxen in Britain

In Britain, the traditional use of oxen for draught fell out of use about the third quarter of the eighteenth century, earlier in some areas, later in others. Draught oxen survived sporadically till 1930-1940 at opposite ends of the country, in some islands of Orkney, and in Sussex, as well as in parts of the mainland of Britain. One team remains to the present day in Gloucestershire. About 1770-1830 came a revival of oxen by improving landlords and wealthy tenant farmers who sought to harness and handle them rather in the manner of horses, but the revival was sporadic and short-lived and failed to displace the horse as the main plough animal. Nevertheless there was much discussion in print on the comparative virtues and economics of oxen and horses, in which the majority of writers, following the thirteenth-century Walter of Henley, came out strongly in favour of oxen.

The British evidence can be divided into four sections:

(a) prehistoric, represented by finds of yokes in peat bogs.

(b) early medieval to eighteenth century, a period in which the ox left its name on a basic unit of land settlement, the oxgang, oxgate, or bovate.

(c) c. 1770-1830, a short-lived revival period after the continuous tradition had been broken.

(d) nineteenth-twentieth century survivals stemming from (c) or more rarely in unbroken line from (b).

This pattern has its own virtues and restrictions for the investigator. On the one hand, it is difficult to get oral information on the handling, training, yoking, and general treatment of oxen, and greater reliance must be placed on the documentary evidence. On the other this limitation means that the British evidence, up to the late eighteenth-early nineteenth century, provides a fixed point against which subsequent changes and innovations in neighbouring areas may be measured. For example, there is no indication that the frame yoke ever reached Britain. This type, with its yoke beam, four struts at right angles, and its straight wooden cross bar underneath, is known over a wide area, including Central Europe and Sweden. The rigidity of the

2

construction made it especially suitable for training young and in-
experienced oxen, which may partly explain its adoption in parts of
Sweden where trading in half-tamed or badly tamed steers was carried
on. It is at any rate the newest type of double yoke to have reached
Sweden, coinciding mainly with areas where draught oxen are of
comparatively recent introduction (Erixon 1957, 32; Hagar 1952, 5-17).
The general use of oxen with yokes for draught ceased in Britain too
early to allow for the diffusion of the frame yoke into the country,
though it is the sort of thing that the improvers might well have
adopted, and this kind of fact may offer a clue in investigations into the
relative antiquity of the frame yoke and head yoke in the various
regions of Europe. As regards yokes, Britain is a relict area.

Two further patterns can be perceived. The first is that the
documentary sources show a geographical distinction between areas of
ox or mixed ox and horse draught, and areas of horse draught. In
historical times, horses alone appear to have been used in the plough
in the Scottish Highlands and Islands (excluding the Northern Isles),
in Ireland, and the Isle of Man. Indeed, in the Highland areas of
Scotland the horse was so firmly entrenched that the term *oxgang*,
referring to a unit of land based on the working capabilities of each
of a team of eight oxen, an eighth of a *ploughgate*, was replaced by the
horsegang, reckoned as the amount of land allotted to each of a team of
four horses, a fourth part of a ploughgate. The equivalence of two oxen
to one horse parallels the state of affairs in, for example, the Slavic
lands east of Germany in the twelfth century, where the ploughland
measure was what could be worked by a pair of oxen or one horse
(White 1964, 63). It may be significant that it is precisely in those areas
of equine predominance that the prehistoric horn yokes for oxen have
been found.

The second pattern, closely linked with the first, is marked by a
change in yoke types. The early yokes from peat bogs in Shetland,
West Scotland, and Ireland are for attachment to the head, with the
possible exception of an Irish group that may be associated with horses
and chariots. The horn yokes must be for oxen, since horses are not
yoked by the head. They are characterised by horizontal perforations,
and knobs and grooves that retained the thongs for tying the yoke to
the horns, and for attaching the pole or beam to the centre of the yoke
(Fig. 9). The documentary evidence from the early Middle Ages,
however, is exclusively for a bow yoke (withers yoke) with vertical
holes in the beam to take the bows that encircled the animals' necks.

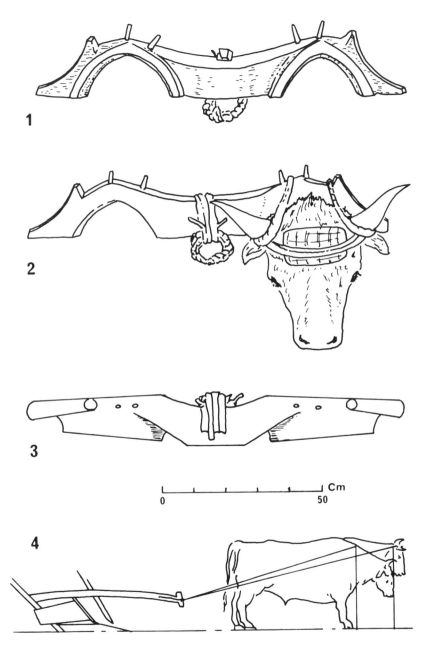

Fig. 1. 1-3. A 'Roman' ox yoke, used by an improver in southern England in 1776; 4. Showing the head and neck positions under the withers yoke and horn yoke. From *Transactions* II (1789), 81, 87.

The use of a Roman ox yoke (Fig. 1, 1-3) for draught by the base of the horns and forehead won a gold medal in 1776 for James Black of Mordon in the South of England, but this was an innovation that has no place in the yoke tradition of historical times in Britain. Indeed, the two old Devonshire oxen in his team of four, having always worn the bow yoke, kept their noses to the ground in their usual manner to let the yoke act on their neck (Fig. 1, 4) and so could not exert all their power under the horn yoke (*Transactions* 1789, 81ff).

The bog finds of horn yokes conform functionally to the type favoured by Black, who was drawing on his experience abroad, and were no doubt attached to the heads of the animals with bands over a protective pad in much the same way (Fig. 1, 2).

The implications of the change in yoke types remain to be explored in detail, and must be set aside meantime. The rest of this study will concentrate on the bow yoke as the standard British type from the early Middle Ages.

Linguistically, the existence of the bow yoke can be ascertained by the words *bow* and *ox bow*, recorded from the fourteenth century in English and from the sixteenth in Scottish sources. Visually, there are manuscript illustrations of fourteenth-century date, such as those in the Luttrell Psalter of c. 1340, and in a manuscript of Langland's *Piers Plowman*, of c. 1380. The former is an early picture of a swing plough drawn by two pairs of oxen yoked one in front of the other, bearing yokes, with bows whose tips penetrate the yoke beam and are clipped together by a band in their pairs. The trace rope runs from the centre of the first yoke to the centre of the second, thence to the muzzle of the plough to which it is attached by a large loop. The 1380 illustration shows a swing-plough drawn by two horned oxen (with horse tails) under a bow yoke. This is a more fanciful picture, and the animals do not have their necks bent to the full in the workmanlike manner of those in the Luttrell Psalter. Other medieval pictures do not provide as clear evidence for yokes, though the bent heads of the pig-like animals pulling what appears to be a wheel ard, in a manuscript of Caedmon's *Paraphrase* (Junius XI), of c. 1000 A.D., are also characteristic of the position adopted under a withers yoke (Steensberg 1936, 263-64, 270-71).

In the seventeenth and eighteenth centuries, the largest group of illustrations occur as ornaments and symbols on the gravestones of farmers in East Central Scotland, often alongside other representations of farming gear such as plough shares and coulters. They date from the

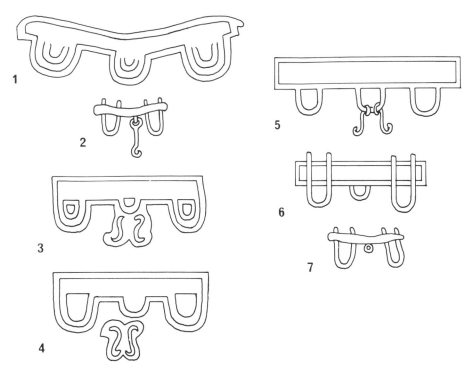

Fig. 2. Ox yokes on tombstones: 1. Kilmadock, Perthshire, 1627; 2. Logie Pert, Angus, 1666; 3-6. Dunblane, Perthshire, 1634, 1652, 1666; 7. Inverarity, Angus, 1756. From Christison XXXVI (1901-2), 296, 308, 410, 411, 415.

1620s to the 1750s, by which time the traditional use of oxen as draught animals was ending. The stone masons who carved the tombstones have produced both symbolic and realistic ox yokes, but all can be seen (Fig. 2) to be bow yokes, with a central attachment, often with two hooks facing in opposite directions, for the chain or rope linking them with the wagon pole or plough beam.

One Scottish bow yoke is said to have been found in a walled-up cupboard in a castle in Aberdeenshire. The yoke beam (Fig. 3) is of oak and measures 3 ft. 8½ in. (113 cm.) long, 4 in. (10 cm.) across, and 2¾ in. (6.4 cm.) thick. At each end is a pair of vertical, oval openings for the bows, and in the centre are two squarish openings, set close together, to take a fastening for holding the draught chain.

The bows that accompany this yoke are of tubular iron, 1⅛ in. (2.7 cm.) diameter, and the inner strut of each bow contains two rectangular openings for retaining pins, so placed as to permit vertical adjustment of 2½ ins. (6.3 cm.).

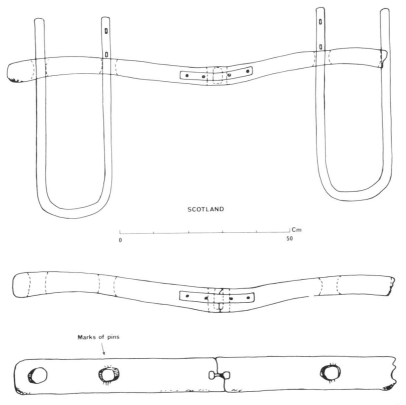

SCOTLAND

Cm

0   50

Marks of pins

Fig. 3. Scottish bow yoke, with bows of iron, possibly the only one to survive in Scotland. On loan to NMAS.

The bows are rather heavy in relation to the lightness of the yoke beam, and may replace wooden bows, which were usually of ash, elm or willow, as in English and Welsh examples (Legge 1905, 222; Payne 1954, 144; Jenkins 1962, 50-51; Hennell 1934, 23). The wooden bows also have their retaining pegs on the inner uprights, and occasionally in both (Fig. 4, 6). The bows of the Devon yoke (Fig. 4, 7) are of solid iron.

The type is uniform throughout Britain, with minor variations. For example, nineteenth-century Sussex and Oxfordshire yokes, instead of having a smoothly curved beam of fairly even thickness throughout, have more shaping about them, and the parts in contact with the animals' necks are curved, so that the outer ends appear to hang down over the outsides of the necks (Legge, 1905, 222; Seebohm 1927, facing 332 and 364) (Fig. 4, 3 and 6). This may be a nineteenth-century sophistication, since a yoke illustrated in 1808 (Young, 1808, 278) (Fig.

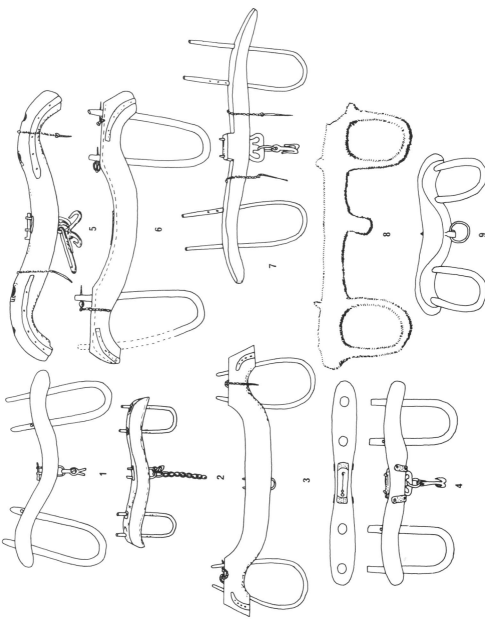

Fig. 4. 1. A Welsh yoke. From Payne, 1944; 2. An early 19th-century yoke from Sussex. From Young, 1808; 3. A late 19th-century yoke from Sussex. From Legge, 1905; 4. From Devonshire. In Holsworthy Museum; 5. From Box, Wiltshire. In MERL; 6. From Wilcote, Oxfordshire, used with white cattle from South Wales (Dynevor breed) up till 1914. In MERL; 7. A yoke with iron bows, from Dean Court, Brickfastleigh, Devon. In MERL; 8. From Gloucestershire. In the Gloucester Folk Museum, 9. From County Down, Northern Ireland. The beam is painted dark blue, and the bows are orange. Said to have been used in breaking in oxen. From a photograph supplied by Dr A. Gailey, Ulster Folk Museum.

4, 2) is not so developed. The downwards curve of the centre of the yoke beam is a feature that distinguishes withers yokes from head yokes.

Such variations as exist (Fig. 4) are comparatively unimportant in that they do not affect the type. Indeed, only one reference has come to hand for a substantially different type of yoke. This, too, was in Sussex, the longest surviving stronghold of the yoke tradition, and was apparently a single yoke used on oxen working in line ahead in particularly wet areas (Young 1808, 280). No description was given, and no examples or illustrations have so far turned up, but considering the strength of the bow tradition, it is likely that these had single bows and resembled the single yokes of, for example, France and Spain (Haudricourt etc. 1955, 121), which are only a step away from becoming collars.

Ox yokes were made by local carpenters, like William Law who produced six for the Monymusk Estate in Aberdeenshire in 1748, at a total cost of 9/- Scots (9d. sterling) (Hamilton 1946, 76). The bows did not require the same degree of skill in making, and according to the Welsh Laws of the tenth century, the driver who accompanied the animals in the plough (as opposed to the actual ploughman) was responsible for furnishing the bows of the yokes, of wythes (Seebohm 1927, 65; Payne 1948, 84-85; Owen 1941, 322-33). It is likely that they were normally made, or at least replaced, when the first set had worn out, by the men on the farms rather than by professional craftsmen.

Teams and Techniques

The number and disposition of animals in a team have varied considerably from the earliest times, and it is unwise to talk of a standard team until the two-horse plough of recent days, though two-animal teams are common in Bronze Age rock engravings and in medieval manuscript illustrations. The picture is complicated by the fact that from shortly after Domesday Book (1086) horses also began to be used in the plough in England, and mixed teams of animals have to be reckoned with from the twelfth to the nineteenth centuries. There has been discussion about the eight ox teams that constituted the *caruca* of the Domesday Book and other medieval documents. This did not necessarily imply a plough drawn by eight oxen all at once, but rather the number required to carry out the agricultural work of a farming unit. Indeed, no medieval manuscript illustration shows a team larger than four. To some extent the eight ox unit comprised two groups of four, with a change over at midday (Richardson 1942, 287-88, 292), paralleling the arrangement in, for example, Northumberland, Nottingham, etc. in the late eighteenth century, where on some farms the ploughmen had teams of four oxen, of which two were used in the morning, and two in the afternoon. In the first decade of the nineteenth century one Scottish farmer kept a team of three oxen, of which no more than two were ever worked at the same time, whereas formerly in plough teams of two oxen plus two horses, an additional two oxen were kept to relieve those in draught (Bailey etc. 1794, 29; Lowe 1794, 50; *Agricultural Mag.* 1811, 227, 235). Instances could easily be multiplied.

This is not to say that eight animal teams were not in use. On the contrary, teams of up to ten were common in twelfth-century Essex and elsewhere, and in North-East Scotland teams of twelve worked on the larger farms until the nineteenth century. Occasionally even bigger numbers were used for specific purposes, for example, a team of sixteen, used in the 1840s in the parish of Cullen, Banffshire to pull a new type of draining plough that made a bed for tile drains (*NSA* 1845, 335). In general, however, team sizes up to the time of the adoption of the two-horse plough ran from four to eight, and occasionally ten, the variations depending on a variety of factors such as local soil types and conditions, plough types, social organisation, the training of young animals, the need to work animals gently to allow them to fatten up for sales, and sometimes, in the case of very large teams, simply for prestige.

It would be tedious to attempt to enumerate the permutations and variations in team sizes and composition for the whole of the country. They are partly summed up by a writer of 1762: 'All the following varieties are used; two horses; three horses; three oxen and one horse; two oxen and two horses; four horses; two oxen and three horses; four oxen and one horse; six oxen; four oxen and two horses; six oxen and one horse; eight oxen; six oxen and one horse; eight oxen; six oxen and two horses; and four oxen and four horses. The four oxen and one horse, or the six oxen and one horse, are only used in a strait, when another horse cannot easily be procured. The custom of using three oxen and one horse, is but lately introduced, and is observed in very few places; every one of the others mentioned is the established custom in some part of the country' (Dickson 1770, I, 244).

To give depth to this general statement, it will be profitable to examine in detail the situation in those areas where oxen survived longest in use.

Orkney, Shetland and Caithness

This area has a special interest since it borders on districts where horses or ponies alone have been used in the plough for half a millennium or more. In all three areas, the team was normally of four or sometimes in Orkney of three animals yoked abreast. In Shetland the team was usually of four oxen abreast, though in the island of Unst four horses, or two horses and two oxen were used, and in Dunrossness four horses, all in similar formation.

In Delting it is specifically mentioned that the oxen had yokes (*OSA* 1791, 391-2), and an illustration of 1822 shows that these were bow yokes of the usual kind. The oxen were so arranged that the inner pair stood half a body's length behind the outer pair, and the two yokes appear to couple the inner pair on the one hand, and the outer pair on the other (Hibbert 1822, Plate 6, Fig. 20). The oxen and cows of Shetland were said in 1733 to be larger than those of Orkney and Caithness (Gifford 1786, 24).

In Orkney much greater emphasis was laid on horses, which worked in teams of two, three or four, still for the most part abreast though the innovation of arranging the animals two by two had come in by the end of the eighteenth century. On occasion cows were linked with horses in the team. In some districts, about 1800 the bow yoke had been replaced by collars and harness. The emphasis on horses in the plough is partly explained by a substantial trade in horses with the North Mainland of Scotland across the Pentland Firth and by the trade in the opposite direction of Orkney cattle, sold to Lowland farmers. Oxen, however, served for other functions like harrowing and transporting peat (*OSA* 1795, 417-18), so reversing the older order.

In Caithness the situation was more mixed, with four oxen or cows, or four horses, being equally used in most parts. Yoking was abreast, but the 'long yoke' of animals two by two had begun to be used in the parish of Halkirk by the 1740s, and in the Force area by the 1780s. One farmer had six ploughs, each drawn by four oxen in the forenoon, and four horses in the afternoon (Fenton 1962-63, 280-3; Wight 1784, 320-1, 363). An estate plan of the lands of Castlehill, near Thurso, dated 1772, incorporates two drawings representing plough teams of four horses two by two, and of four oxen abreast (Megaw 1962, 218-23, Plates x-xi). As usual, there is one man to control the plough, and another to drive the animals. The oxen, like the horses, are harnessed by collars and traces, and stand in an equal line unlike the staggered arrangement of the four yoked oxen in Hibbert's 1822 illustration from Shetland.

This staggering is due to the fact that 'a large yoke is laid on the neck of the two outermost, and a small yoke on the innermost oxen. These yokes are joined by a double rope, to the middle of which is fixed the draught or chain, which is from 24 to 18 feet long, from the neck of the oxen to the nose of the plough' (*OSA* 1793, 585). In the Shetland dialect the short yoke borne by the inner oxen was the *skammyok*, and the long one for the outer oxen the *ootyok*.

Such a method of yoking may also have been used in early medieval Wales, where, according to the tenth-century laws, there were yokes of four lengths, the *beriau* or short yoke, four feet long, the *mei-iau* or middle yoke, eight feet long, the *ceseiliau* or arm-pit yoke, twelve feet long, and the *hiriau* or long yoke, sixteen feet long. The first two would equate with the short and long Shetland yokes, and the others must have been for teams of six and eight oxen abreast. The National Museum of Ireland has a broken example (Fig. 9, 12), originally 7 ft. (213 cm.) long.

The recent find of a wooden head yoke with Iron Age analogues (Fig. 9, 2) indicates the existence of draught oxen in Shetland at an early period. The earliest documentary sources refer without exception to four ox teams, and linguistic evidence suggests that plough teams both in Orkney and Shetland were of oxen, not horses, in earlier times. In Orkney, the four horses were named, from right to left facing them, the *fur-horse*, the *fur-scam*, the *volar scam*, and the *outend horse*, the first two walking on the ploughed land, the second two on the unploughed land. The words *volar* and *scam*, from Old Norse *vǫllr*, a field, and *skammr*, short, can only be properly understood if it is assumed that the terms have at some stage been transferred from oxen to horses. The *fur-scam* and *volar scam* may then be thought of as the pair of oxen linked by the *skammyok*, one the short-yoke ox going in the furrow, the other the short-yoke ox going on the land (Fenton 1962-3, 287).

In the Northern Isles and Caithness, therefore, in the eighteenth century and well through the nineteenth, an age-old draught-ox tradition is being or has been replaced by horses, especially in Orkney. The change was presumably hastened by the trade in 1-2 year old horses from Sutherland, Ross-shire, and Caithness, carried on with Orkney till about 1830 (*OSA* 1793, 339; *Old Lore Misc.* 1909, 192-3, and 1910, 74-75; Sinclair 1795, 96), but it must also represent the tail end of the change-over from oxen (as indicated by finds of early head yokes) to horses as draught-animals, in what may be characterised as the area of four animals abreast. This area stretches as far south as Wales, where the team of four oxen abreast survived until the fourteenth, and sporadically until the sixteenth century (Payne 1954, 85, 109; Richards 1954, 137). One may hazard a guess, therefore, that the nucleus of the change lies somewhere in Western Britain, and antedates at least the sixteenth century in Scotland when such references as can be found are to horse ploughs (Munro 1961, 80). In seventeenth-century Ireland there were a number of official edicts against the attachment of horses by the tail to the short plough. A report to King Charles, dated soon after 1612, recommended that men should 'furnish themselves with such Ploughs as are in use in England, or learn to use their short Ploughs, setting their Garrons three or four Horses affront, which is free from unseemliness, & fitter for some mountaines & boggish grounds than the long Plough, as is now begun & practized in the Barony of Clankie, in the Countie of Cavan' (*UJA* 1856, 171; 1857, 164; 1858, 215). Though bullocks were also spoken of as yoked by the tail, it is clear that horses were the main plough animals by the early seventeenth century in Ireland. The replacement of oxen by horses therefore appears to be a development, no doubt started well before the sixteenth century, that took place in Western Britain and Ireland, and was still in progress in the Northern Isles and Caithness in the late eighteenth and early nineteenth centuries, when it was cancelled out by an entirely new set of factors, diffused from Lowland Scotland in the train of the Agricultural Revolution.

Recent History

The use of oxen in the plough, harrow, and cart lingered on into the twentieth century in the Northern Isles. A single ox or a pair continued until shortly after 1900 to draw the light single-stilted plough that survived alongside improved two-horse types for earthing up potatoes and giving a final ploughing before a barley crop. They were harnessed with collars, traces, and a swingle-tree, and were sometimes controlled by the ploughman using reins, sometimes by a second man leading them. A backband of leather or twisted straw, or of rope, helped to support the traces.

The halter or bridle on the animal's face consisted of a pair of wooden cheek pieces, each pierced by two horizontal openings, and a vertical one. From the vertical openings a rope, called the *head stool*, passed over the head. A *nose band* linked the foremost opening in each cheekpiece, and a *choke-band* did the same at the back, under the ox's throat. When the oxen were working in pairs they were linked by a rope looped through the nose band of each halter. Occasionally the oxen had iron bits of light construction that did not go through their mouths in the same manner as horses' bits, but curved across the fronts of their noses, replacing the nose band.

Whether they pulled a single-stilted plough or a harrow, or a flagstone used for clod crushing, this was the form of harnessing in the nineteenth and early twentieth centuries (Fenton 1962-63, Plates XLVII, 1-2, XLVIII, 2). The beginnings of the change from yokes to collars can be dated back to the end of the eighteenth century for plough oxen. Oxen were also used for drawing carts and wagons, and it is conceivable that the use of oxen between a pair of shafts was instrumental in furthering the change. In 1721 John Traill of Elsness in Sandness, Orkney had amongst his possessions six oxen for carts (Marwick 1939, 22). An inventory of the implements on the estate of the improving landlord, Sir James Stewart of Burray, included one ox wagon and part of another. There was also a horse wain, showing that the pulling of four-wheeled wagons was not the prerogative of oxen (Marwick 1934, 47-54). In 1814 small two-wheeled box carts drawn by two oxen or one horse were common in Orkney, and some of the gentlemen farmers had larger carts (Shirreff 1814, 53). They had clearly been diffused by the practice of the innovating landlords and taken over by the ordinary farmers who had recognised their value for carrying manure, peats, etc. In Shetland at the same date carts were rare, and everything had to be carried on horseback or on the backs of the people themselves. A few small ox wagons were employed, mainly on the farms of landed proprietors (*Ibid.*, 36), as in Orkney until a few years previously. By the 1870s, small carts drawn by ponies, or more rarely by oxen, had also become common in Shetland (Cowie 1879, 159).

Ox carts remained in service until the 1940s. Most of the photographic illustrations come from Fair Isle, with some from the island of Fetlar, from the Whiteness and Weisdale area of Mainland Shetland, and from Hoy and one or two other parts of Orkney. They date between about 1910 and 1940, and in every case the oxen are harnessed exactly as for horses, with a collar and harness, breeching straps, a small saddle with a crub to hold the back chains or back band, and a belly band. Some of the collars are well made of leather, with narrow iron hames, others are crudely made of coils of straw sewn around with hessian from old sacks, and often with wooden harness. They are usually open at one end so that they can be slipped easily over the animal's neck.

In the North Isles of Orkney, for example Stronsay, Eday, and Westray, there appear to have been larger carts pulled by two oxen in the late eighteenth century, although these did not survive long into the nineteenth century. As recently as the 1920s there could still be seen in Rousay carts with two small spoked wheels pulled by two oxen attached to a pole. According to a Westray man, they were linked to the pole by a wooden yoke in the time of his grandmother, about 1860 (Simpson 1963, 157).

The question of the four-wheeled wains that in the eighteenth and early nineteenth-century references are associated with the farms of proprietors is of exceptional interest since a vehicle of corresponding type was at work in the islands of Graemsay, Hoy, and Flotta, in Orkney, until the 1940s, and in Flotta until 1950, when the last ox on the island died. Locally, they are known as *sleds*, *coaches*, *hurleys*, or *lorries*, the word *sled* being commonest. The small wheels, less than two feet in diameter, may be solid, or may have four sturdy spokes. Some of the surviving solid wheels have been cut from old ships' hatches (Fenton 1978, 323).

These *sleds* may not be the lineal descendants of the eighteenth-century wains, since the name *sled* suggests the comparatively recent addition of wheels to a sledge with runners. The first wheeled *sled* in Graemsay is said to have been made only about 1910, the idea for it having come from Rackwick in Hoy. The method of attachment of the draught animals is also reminiscent of a sledge, the trace ropes being as a rule linked to hooks or loops on the front outer corners of the *sleds*. On occasion the link-up is by traces and swingle tree (Fox 1931, 198, Plate XVI). One Graemsay example was fitted with a turntable and pole, due to the influence of a man familiar with the prairie wagons of the United States. In no case is there any record of yokes being used with the oxen that drew the sleds, and all descriptions and photographs indicate a collar, backband, and traces, as for oxen in the plough or harrow.

North-East Scotland

Oxen remained in longer and more consistent use in North-East Scotland than in most other parts of Britain, with the possible exception of Sussex. Material extracted from the Statistical Accounts of the 1790s and the 1840s throws interesting light on the state of affairs at these periods.

Table 1. *Plough Teams in Aberdeenshire*

Name of Parish (H = hilly, L = low-lying)	1790	1845
Alford H	346 plough oxen, 65 ploughs. Teams of 12 and 10 oxen, some 8 and under. Also mixtures of oxen, horses, bulls, cows, young cattle (smaller tenants).	112 ploughs, drawn by 2 oxen or 2 horses. Teams of 4 oxen for breaking in.
Auchindoir H	10-12 oxen. 2 horses plus 4-6 small oxen and cows.	
Auchterless L	14 ploughs drawn by oxen, and 2, or 3-4 horses.	4 horses for breaking in.
Birse H	120 ploughs. Mixed oxen, cattle, horses. Collars on oxen.	
Bourtie L	Many use 10-ox ploughs.	
Cluny H/L	10-12 oxen with yokes and wooden bows. Landlords use 2 horses plus 4 oxen, or sometimes 2 up to 10 or 12 oxen with collars and traces.	
Crimond L	Formerly 6 horses, or 10-12 oxen. Now 4 horses or 4 oxen, sometimes 2 horses.	79 ploughs, a few ox drawn.
Drumoak L	Oxen less used than formerly.	
Echt L/H	53 Old Scotch ploughs, 5 small English ploughs. 6, 8 or 10 oxen. 4 oxen plus 2 horses. 2 oxen (1 plough). 2 horses (3 ploughs). 4 horses (5-6 ploughs).	
Fintry L	Number of oxen down by half since horses came in.	

Name of Parish (H = hilly, L = low-lying)	1790	1845
Forbes and Kearn H	8, 10 and 12 oxen. Some mixed teams of oxen and horses.	
Fraserburgh L	Formerly 6-8 oxen, now 2 horses. Horses were fewer in number, but bigger.	
Fyvie L	8, 10 or 12 oxen. 4 horses. 2 horses plus 2 oxen.	
Huntly H	Ordinary tenants yoke horses and cattle together.	
Keig H	47 ploughs, with 88 horses, 87 cows, 153 oxen and young cattle. Neighbours often join in making a team.	
Keith Hall and Kinkell L	In 1778, 26 ploughs drawn by 10-12 oxen. Now (1794) only 8 ploughs drawn by 10 oxen each. Number of horses (and horse drawn ploughs) has increased.	
King Edward L	135 ploughs, of which 15 are drawn by oxen, 76 by 2 horses, 44 by 4 horses.	
Kinnellar L	25 ploughs, of which 7 are drawn by oxen and cows (4-10 in a team), 18 by horses.	
Kintore L	Only one farmer still uses 4 horses plus 2 cattle (on a rocky, stony soil).	
Leochel-Cushnie H	4-12 oxen. Small farmers yoke cows and young cattle.	2 horses or 2 oxen. 104 horses, 18 oxen.
Leslie H	22 ploughs, drawn by 8, 10, or 12 oxen. 5-6 of these drawn by mixed horses and oxen. 1 plough drawn by 2 horses.	
Logie Coldstone H	Richest tenants, 12 oxen, others 10-18 oxen. Poorer ones, 2 horses plus 2 cows, some 1 horse, 2 cows, and 2 small oxen.	
Lonmay L		4 oxen or 4 horses for trench ploughing.

Name of Parish (H = hilly, L = low-lying)	1790	1845
Lumphanan H	44 ploughs, 8-10 oxen. There are 56 ploughgates, but sometimes 2-3 unite and are ploughed by 10 oxen.	
Meldrum L	4 horses or 4 oxen (autumn and winter). 2 horses or 2 oxen (spring — a lighter plough). A few 8-10 ox teams (Old Scotch plough).	
Methlick L	50 ploughs, mostly ox drawn.	
Midmar H	132 horses, 525 black cattle, 59 ploughs, 91 carts.	
New Deer L	230 ploughs on 80 old ploughgates. 712 horses, 3200 cattle.	
Newhills L	88 ploughs, of which 49 were drawn by horses (2-3 in a team), 7 by oxen, the rest by mixed teams.	
New Machar L	68 ploughs, of which 3 are drawn by 10 oxen, 1 by 8 oxen, 5 by 4 oxen, 3 by 2 horses plus 2 oxen, 3 by 4 horses, 6 by 2 horses, 47 by 2 horses plus 4 black cattle.	
Old Deer L	2 horses. 4-6 with collars.	
Oyne H	46 ploughs.	Old 10 ox ploughs made furrows 16″ wide and often 16″ deep.
Peterculter L	10-12 small oxen, under yoke. 4 horses. 6-8 oxen plus horses. A few 2 horses or 2 oxen, with reins and no driver.	
Peterhead L	A few 2 horse or 2 ox ploughs. 4-6 horses for old Scotch plough, often 2 horses plus a cow and a young steer, and sometimes a horse, cow, and young steer. About 90 ploughs.	4 oxen or 4 horses for trenching.

Name of Parish (H = hilly, L = low-lying)	1790	1845
Rayne L	Large farms: 8-10 oxen. Crofts: 2 horses, or 2 horses plus 2 cows.	
Slains L	4-6 horses. 4, 6, 10 or 12 oxen. Sometimes mixed oxen and horses.	
Strathdon H	170 ploughs, drawn by 8, 10, or 12 oxen, sometimes oxen and horses together, sometimes horses alone. Rich farmers use 2 horses with reins and no driver. In Corgarff, 4 horses abreast.	Bucharn had 6 ploughs, 18 horses, and 6 yokes of 10-12 cattle, c. 1800; now has 3 ploughs, 4 horses, and a pair or sometimes 2 pairs of oxen.
Tarland H	3-4 horses. 8, 10 or 12 oxen.	
Tarves L	10-12 oxen. 4-6 horses.	
Tough H	2-3 small crofters often join to make up a yoke.	
Towie H	43 ploughs, drawn by 8-10 oxen.	78 ploughs drawn by 2 horses.
Tullynessie H	30-40 ploughs. Large farms: 8-10 small oxen. Small farms: small steers, or a mixture of cows and horses.	
Udny L	20 farmers use a 10 ox plough. 10-11 farmers a 6-8 ox plough. Others use 4 horses, or 2-4 cattle plus 2 horses. 87 ploughs.	

This table shows clearly the considerable range of differences possible in a county containing both highland and lowland areas, and with a mixture of farm sizes — a few large farms run by the lairds and richer farmers, a great number of medium-sized and small farms, and several crofts or small holdings of only a few acres. The 1790s column also pinpoints a stage in the diffusion of innovations in harnessing and equipment. In the upland western extremities it links up with the area

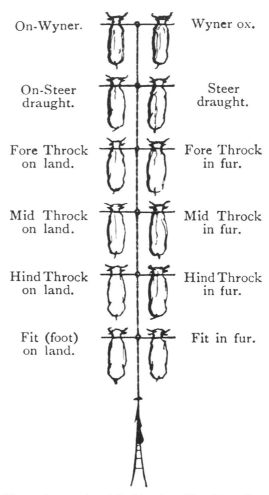

On-Wyner.   Wyner ox.

On-Steer   Steer
draught.   draught.

Fore Throck   Fore Throck
on land.   in fur.

Mid Throck   Mid Throck
on land.   in fur.

Hind Throck   Hind Throck
on land.   in fur.

Fit (foot)   Fit in fur.
on land.

Fig. 5. The twelve-ox plough in Aberdeenshire. From Pratt, 1858.

of four horses abreast, for example in the Corgarff district of
Strathdon. On the lower-lying lands, however, oxen were in the
majority for pulling the plough, except on some large farms in more
prosperous districts where the improved ploughs of the period had
brought in the fashion of yoking only a pair of horses, controlled by the
ploughman with reins, and without a driver.

The very large team of twelve oxen, unknown or rare in other parts
of the country, was worked on large farms in nearly every parish of
Aberdeenshire, though by the 1790s it was becoming less prevalent,
partly because the number of oxen in the county was on the decrease at

this time. It is often said by the ministers who wrote the entries in the Statistical Accounts that the team of twelve was a mark of social prestige, and no doubt it was in part since human nature is irrepressible. However, there was more to it than mere pomp, as appears from an examination of the structure of the twelve-ox team.

The layout is shown in the accompanying diagram (Fig. 5), in which the individual oxen are named (Pratt 1870, 20).

In one source the names are given in pairs, in the form of a crude rhyme:

> Fit yoke
> Hin frock
> Fore frock
> Mid yoke
> Steer draught o' laan,
> Wyners (Gregor 1881, 179).

The bow yokes over the necks of the oxen were linked by a trace rope or chain known as a *soam*. The rear end was hooked into an iron staple fixed on the right-hand side of the plough beam, some little distance back from the point, or to a bridle at the tip of the beam. The trace was fastened to each of the yokes by a staple through the centre of the yoke beam, and a ring and hooks. In addition, the *fit owsen* (foot oxen) had a short series of elongated links, known as *staffs*, attached to the ring, and by means of these links the trace rope or chain could be raised and lowered to give the plough more or less depth as required. The *fit o' lan'* (foot on land) ox was not considered fully trained until it had learned to lower its neck when the ploughman cried 'Jouk!' (duck) so as to let the plough go a little deeper at that particular moment.

The yokes, usually of oak, were equipped with bows of ash, birch, or willow, whose points penetrated the yoke beam and were pinned above. A pad of dried rushes, straw, or strips of bog fir roots was set between the neck of the oxen and the bow to prevent grazing due to the pressure of unyielding wood.

The most important oxen in the team were the foot oxen, nearest the plough, and the *wyners* (*wyne* = to turn) at the front. Similarly in Wales the best and strongest oxen, the *ychen bon*, 'root or base oxen', were in pairs nearest the plough, and the furrow ox, *rychor*, was required to be better trained than the land ox or *gwelltor* (*rhych* = furrow, *gwellt* = grass) (Richards 1954, 136-7). A good *wyner* was frequently kept till ten or twelve years old since on him depended the smooth turning of the long team at the end of the furrow, and the general steadiness of movement. Immediately behind them in the *steer-draught* (*steer* = young bullock) came the young oxen undergoing training, for whose discipline the *wyners* were in part responsible. The foot oxen, being nearest the plough, had the most immediate effect on its motion, and had to be trained accordingly. The rest lent their strength to the team, which could be reduced to ten by removing the *mid-throcks* (Pratt 1870, 20-1; Gregor 1881, 179-81; Alexander 1877, 33-37). With these and the trainee oxen away, the team of eight remained, and it is evident from the table above that teams of eight and ten were much more common than the large team of twelve. It can be seen, however, that the question of training came into the composition of the teams, and this must be borne in mind as well as the prestige element.

Where horses formed part of the team, the total strength rarely exceeded six, and the horses always preceded the oxen, in pairs. This arrangement can be seen on a tombstone dated 1753-1754 in Liberton Churchyard, Edinburgh, and was widespread in Lowland Scotland. It is possible that the practical difficulties of harnessing a pair of horses with collars in front of one or two pairs of yoked oxen was a strong factor in bringing about the change from ox yokes to ox collars in the last two decades of the eighteenth century, in England and Wales as well as in Scotland. Where horses alone were used in the old Scotch plough, six were reckoned as equal to ten-twelve oxen.

As long as ploughs required fairly large teams, it was impossible for the smaller farmers and crofters to maintain individually the necessary animal power, and this meant that they had to make do with such beasts as they had. As a result, alongside the sturdy teams of eight, ten, or twelve oxen, or six horses, or two horses and four oxen, or latterly four horses or four oxen, or the two-horse (rarely two-ox), driverless teams of the new plough types, there could be seen motley crews of animals, mixtures of oxen, horses, bulls, cows, and young beasts, averaging four in number but also occurring in odd numbers, such as three, composed of a horse, cow, and young steer (Peterhead), and five, composed of a horse, two cows, and two small oxen (Logie Coldstone).

In addition, to make up these teams, it was necessary for two or more small tenants to *neighbour*, or work together with each other, so reflecting the needs of an earlier tradition of joint-farming under the run-rig system. It was quite a formal system, of long standing, that had on occasion to be enforced by the local Baron Court, as when it was ordained in 1678 that William Menie in Castle Forbes should 'stryk (unite) oxen in a plewch with James Duncain, and sall bear good neighbourhood with him, wnder the payne of ten libs' (Forbes 1919, 318).

Collaterally with the decreases in numbers of oxen that marked the improving standards of agriculture, there went an increase in the number of horses and sometimes of two-horse ploughs. Alford had ploughs drawn by 346 oxen and an unstated number of horses in the 1790s. By 1845 there were 112 ploughs each drawn by two horses or two oxen, a total of 224 animals. In Drumoak oxen were less used than formerly in the 1790s, and in Fintry they had been reduced by half since horses began to be used in the plough. Towie had 43 ploughs drawn by eight-ten oxen in the 1790s, and 78 ploughs drawn by two horses each in 1845. This is a development, of course, that was common to the whole country, and it must be regarded as an important aspect of the capitalisation of farming, with a considerable bearing on the reduction in size of labour units on farms, since where each team had formerly required both a ploughman and a driver, now the ploughman was enough.

North-East Scotland at the end of the eighteenth century, therefore, was in a state of flux. As elsewhere, the changes were initiated by improving lairds and gentlemen farmers, of whom one of the most notable in Aberdeenshire was Sir Archibald Grant of Monymusk. From the Monymusk Estate Papers a valuable check can be got on the situation prior to the widespread adoption of improved plough types from Northern England and Southern Scotland, against which the range of late eighteenth-century changes can be measured. Probably the commonest size of plough team here in 1749-1750 was ten oxen, and teams of eight oxen, and of four horses plus two oxen, were also frequent. Teams varied in size from ten down to two animals, depending on the nature of the soil in which they were working. There are references to six oxen plus two horses ploughing fallow ground, eight oxen working turnip ground, two horses ploughing in the intervals of the cabbage (previously well worked ground), three horses amongst the turnips, and so on. Variation in team size in relation to soil and crops is not brought out at all in the Old Statistical Account, and the table above, based on this source, must present an altogether too simplified picture that remains to be corrected and filled in by detailed study of local estate papers.

As regards the relationship between implements and man and animal power, a Memorandum of about 1744 notes that 310 bolls (1860 bushels) of grain in tillage should be managed by five ploughs powered by thirty oxen and ten horses, with thirteen servants, and in 1746 it was thought that for a farm worked by four ploughs, the numbers required were twenty oxen, ten horses, and nine persons.

Oxen were also used on the estate for transport. There were wains pulled by six or four oxen, and sturdy wooden sledges, known as *puddocks*, for moving heavy loads of building stone, etc., requiring eight or six oxen. Two-wheeled carts were drawn by two horses, one in front of the other (Hamilton, 1946, 76-127; Hamilton 1945, 143, 146).

In every case, the oxen on the estate wore wooden yokes, and there must normally have been a pad between the bow and the animal's neck since on 24th August, 1749, three men spent a third of a day making ropes and *cods* ('pillows') for oxen.

Four-wheeled wains have already been noted in Orkney and Shetland, and now in Aberdeenshire. They were also known in Morayshire, where oxen are described in 1811 as yoked abreast in a wain with a pole drawn by the necks, in bows connected by a yoke (Leslie 1811, 311), and in Banffshire, where in 1812 a pair of oxen sometimes went abreast in a cart, connected by a pretty heavy yoke (Souter 1812, 257). In the Morayshire reference plough oxen were at the same time harnessed like horses. These and other occurrences of wains (in Angus, Fife, Galloway, etc.) are, however, on the farms of lairds and gentlemen who could afford to keep the numbers of animals needed to pull them, and they did not survive the general disuse of oxen brought about by the Agricultural Revolution.

Recent History

As can be seen from Table 1, oxen had practically disappeared from the farming scene by the mid-nineteenth century, though they still found favour on large farms where teams of four were used for heavy work like trench-ploughing and land reclamation, and of two where theorists thought them more economical and steadier than horses. Lord Kames may here be allowed to speak for his many predecessors, contemporaries, and successors: 'There is not in agriculture any other improvement that equals the using of oxen instead of horses: they are equally tractable; and they are purchased and maintained at much less expense. As this improvement is obvious to the meanest capacity, one might expect to see every farmer greedily embracing it, as he would a feast after being famished. Yet few stir. How is this to be accounted for? Men are led by custom in chains; and in instances without number are fettered against their interest' (Kames 1776, 26-27).

The future did not live up to his oratory, and the horse prevailed. Nevertheless, it is to theorists like this (most of whom were also practical farmers) that the continued sporadic use of oxen in Aberdeenshire as well as elsewhere in Britain must be attributed.

Some later examples may be given. In 1853, John Mackie, farmer at Chapelkirk in the parish of Methlick, bought a pair of oxen at Ellon Market, and used them for ploughing (he also had two pairs of horses), for sledging stones off the fields, and for harrowing (Mackie 1853). In 1870, James Allan ploughed upland on the Battlefield of Harlaw, near Inverurie, into narrow sixteen-foot-wide ridges, sometimes using a pair of strong oxen in preference to horses. 'The yoke or wooden pole over their necks made them hang their heads; the yoke was fixed to the horns, and round the neck, and was attached in the centre to the soam or plough rope. But many oxen wore collars and "hames" like horses, with a common swingletree fitted to the plough' (Allan 1927, 31-32). By this time, the use of a yoke was exceptional.

In the late nineteenth and twentieth centuries, a few examples have come to hand of small farmers who made up their full plough team by

Fig. 6. An ox and horse harnessed together in a pair of harrows, at Claymires, Ordiquhill, Banffshire, 1896. Per Mrs I. McWhirr. C 294.

B

Fig. 7. Iron 'branks' for a cow. From Aberdeenshire. In NMAS (no PN31).

yoking a horse with an ox, cow, or steer (Fig. 6). Leslie Jaffray at Ardoyne, Insch, did so, and noted that the draught of the ox was further up the shoulder than the horse. In the parish of Cruden, about 1920, two small farmers worked their holdings with a horse and steer. The ox had a leather stall collar or *branks* on its head, and wore a collar resembling a horse collar upside down. The same collar was used for carting, along with a saddle and breeching straps. About the same period in the parish of Methlick, another farmer did all his work with steers or a horse and steer, using an open collar that dropped straight down over the steer's neck. The hames fitted into the groove on the collar, and were fastened together at the bottom with a chain that kept both collar and hames firmly in place. The steer's bridle or *branks* consisted of a curved bar of iron about ¾ in. (1.9 cm.) broad that went round its face about 6 in. (15 cm.) above the nostrils, and was jointed in the middle (Fig. 7). Two rings were attached, one on each side of the hinge. The ends of the bar had holes through which a medium-sized rope could run, knotted through one side, passed through the other, and knotted through the ring on the nearside front. This provided a lever for turning and controlling the steer. The other ring, on the front offside, was for coupling the two animals together. A leather strap attached to the centre of each side of the bar passed over the steer's head just behind its ears, and held the *branks* in position. Steers were heavy to handle when turning. They were very strong, and slower but steadier than horses. 'I have seen them stepping up and down the rigs, chewing the cud all the time.' One of the last examples of the use of a cow and mare together was near Stonehaven, south of Aberdeen, in the 1940s (oral information).

Sussex

If Aberdeenshire holds the Scottish record for the number of oxen in a team, so Sussex must hold the British record since here they could go as high as fourteen, an 'uncommonly great' number, as Arthur Young remarked. Larger teams have been known in other parts of the world, for example in the Danish Island of Læsø where, as a result of the tightly organised community system, up to sixteen horses might be employed (Nielsen 1924, 55). In Sussex not the community system but the practicalities of fattening cattle for sale dictated the size of the team, for the farmers thought that if, in a small team, the oxen had continually to exert their full strength, they would not fatten so well. A team of fourteen was exceptional, however, and the more normal number in the late eighteenth century was eight, or ten-twelve in stiff land. Horses, on the other hand, went four in a plough, and never less than three except for the few driverless two-horse ploughs that were beginning to displace the old wheel ploughs (like the Kentish turn-wrest) in the same places. One writer pointed out that the number of oxen was diminishing as hard roads increased, and horses were wanted for long carriages on them (Marshall 1798, 134).

By the end of the eighteenth century, developments had already been taking place in the make up of teams, as elsewhere in Britain, and the emphasis began to lie increasingly on horse teams. Already in the thirteenth century Sussex wagons might be drawn by two oxen and one horse, or by four oxen if no horse was available (Wilson 1959, 110), but oxen were far and away in the majority for draught purposes. About the year 1400 on the Earl of Arundel's farms in East Sussex there were only 34 horses to 211 oxen, not counting steers, bulls, etc., and in West Sussex 33 horses to 237 oxen, oxen being valued at 12/-, but no horse or mare at more than 6/8 (Salzman 1953, 38-39, 40). In the mid-sixteenth century oxen were still the main and sometimes the only draught animals, for example on the property of Sir John Gage of West Firle who, when he died in 1556, had three ox carts, four ploughs and their irons, sixteen draught yokes, four 'nib' yokes (possibly heavy yokes for use in drawing wagons, since the term *nib* has at the present day the sense of a wagon pole in the Sussex and Somerset dialects), and a stock of 24 working oxen. His inventory makes no reference to horses (Fussell 1952, 67). In Oxfordshire at the same period the inventories of the goods of 92 farmers show that only five relied entirely on oxen, and that 37 used horses alone (Havinden 1965, 38), and since early seventeenth-century Sussex references indicate that horses were then well established for draught, it is likely that they were used there, as in Oxfordshire, in the preceding century, at least in certain areas such as the coastal zone. Nevertheless there remained a strong stress on oxen, and the available evidence gives the impression that they were much more consistently worked in Sussex than in contemporary Oxfordshire and many other counties. Thus, John Aridge of Iford, in 1612, had one plough, eight oxen, and two horses; James Stillwell, in 1677, had six oxen and ten horses; C. Humphrey, Newhaven, a yeoman who died in 1697, had two ploughs, one horse, three mares, four oxen, six steers, and six yokes.

In the eighteenth century, many oxen were still used for draught about Rye in the 1770s. There, they were worked only till about five or six years old, before being fattened for the market. As a rule oxen pulled the foot plough, and horses the old one-wheeled plough, in teams of eight and four respectively (Fussell 1952, 68, 72-3, 77-9, 82).

The most comprehensive description of the yoking and working of oxen in Sussex in the late eighteenth-early nineteenth century is given in the writings of Marshall and Young. The oxen were worked in pairs, with bow yokes (Fig. 4, 2-3) except for a few harnessed with collars by 'intelligent individuals', as Young approvingly called them. Training was done by yoking steers in the double yoke, using a rope to confine them, and often a pair of old, steady oxen in front and another behind. Once accustomed to the yoke they were put in the plough, and started work at the age of 2½-3 years. Sometimes a young steer was yoked alongside a steady experienced one. They were worked gently at first and throughout their working life so as not to retard their growth, which continued till they were about six or seven years old. Thus the large teams were intended to ease the individual burden.

In particularly wet areas the oxen were yoked in line ahead — a custom known in many parts of England, though rare in Scotland — and in Sussex, at least, a particular kind of yoke is said to have been used for the single oxen.

In harrowing narrow ridges where the soil was too moist to stand treading, a long, sliding yoke was used, by which the oxen, working abreast, drew in the interfurrows. So that the length would match the varying widths of the ridges, it was made of two pieces of wood, linked by two large staples, moving in long sliding mortices that passed along the middle of each piece. The crowns of the staples reached through the mortices and were so fixed as to give free play to the sliders by means of keys or strong wooden pins. Each slider had a draught iron attached a few inches from the inner bow hole, with a chain or trace passing from it to the harrow, or pair of harrows, that curved over the ridge of the narrow land between the oxen.

An ox team could plough for nine months in the year, whereas a horse team could achieve an acre a day all the year round. On the average, an ox team of eight and a horse team of four were required for the work of a 100-acre farm more or less according to the type of soil (Marshall 1798, 138-9; Young 1793, 77-80, 82; Young 1808, 66, 276-84).

In Sussex it appears that ox bows were home-made, as in Aberdeenshire, and they rarely or never figure in the inventories, as yoke beams do. Some skill was evidently required in their making, since Thomas Marchant noted in his diary for 28 February 1721 that he 'was at William Nicholas's in the morning, teaching him how to make ox bows' (Turner 1873, 189).

A stock list for Kirdford in 1798 showed that though the cattle-fattening industry was flourishing, the numbers of draught oxen were clearly on the decline, so that out of 68 farmers listed only 19 had draught oxen, though all had draught horses, which were twice as numerous as oxen. The desuetude of oxen progressed faster in East Sussex than in West Sussex, and stock totals for 1801 showed in the former 1630 oxen and 9516 horses, in the latter 6668 oxen and 881 horses (Kenyon 1950, 61, 70-71). Though being eroded, the ox tradition was clearly still strong, and the survival of ox teams, usually of six animals, well into the twentieth century must be due not only to the interest of landowners, but also in part to the strength of this tradition. Up till 1913, a dozen or more teams were at work on Sussex farms, ploughing, carting, and harrowing, with sturdy wooden bow yokes over their shoulders, wearing muzzles of net or, earlier, of wicker (Marshall 1798, 136; Legge 1905, 221-3; Seebohm 1927, 306, Fig. 68 facing 332, Fig. 70 facing 362, 364; Hennell 1934, 23), as also in the Weald of Kent. One of the last teams was owned by Major and Mrs Harding, of Birling Manor, near Eastbourne. It was finally given up in 1929.

Elsewhere in England, even by the mid-nineteenth century, survivals were sporadic and almost entirely confined to estates or very large farms, such as Holkham Park and Castleacre Farm in West Norfolk, and Teddesley in Staffordshire (Caird 1852, 166-8, 242). The last occurrences of oxen have not been collected for England as a whole, but in Cornwall it was 1887, in Somerset about 1890, and at Bishopstone in Wiltshire in 1920. The only remaining team is maintained by Lord Bathurst at Cirencester Park in Gloucestershire.

The Change from Yokes to Collars

In Scotland the earliest references to the use of collars and traces on oxen date to the late 1760s (Dickson 1770, 257), and the change is strictly contemporary with the spread of new and improved plough types, though by no means confined to plough teams. By 1773 some improving landlords were using collars in Angus and Fife, and by the end of the decade they occurred in most counties, though chiefly in the Lowlands. At Craigie, near Dundee, oxen were harnessed with collars and traces three in a line in winter, and in pairs in summer when the ground was dry. In other parts of Angus, teams of up to six harnessed oxen drew the plough, and two or four pulled wagons loaded with lime or marl for fertilising the soil. They were rarely shod, except when used on rough roads, in stony areas, or on very moist ground. At Glasserton in Galloway, Admiral Keith Stewart ploughed with harnessed oxen, without a driver. His efforts were praised highly by A. Wight, who observed that in a breeding county like Galloway there was no point in keeping oxen idle, when two years in the plough would do them no harm. In Aberdeenshire, Mr Fraser of Strichen drew a wagon loaded with 256 stones of oatmeal for nine miles along a good road, using four harnessed oxen, shod on their forefeet only. By the 1780s, collars for oxen were well established from Galloway up to Morayshire on the bigger farms (from Wight 1778-84).

The 1790s, as indicated by the Old Statistical Account, and the contemporary Agricultural Surveys, show a reversal of the old order. It is now the yoke that begins to be rare, and questions of social stratification make their appearance, for yokes now tend to be confined to the 'poorer sort', and are described as old-fashioned. By this time, too, the ox as a working animal was almost unknown in several counties. The use of the yoke disappeared along with the ox. With the use of collars came a spasmodc revival of oxen, at first on estate farms, but latterly on small farms after horses had completely ousted even the revivalist ox on the bigger places.

The English and Welsh evidence parallels the Scottish fairly closely. The Agricultural Surveys of the 1790s show that in most districts gentlemen farmers were introducing or re-introducing oxen as draught animals with collars except in areas like Sussex where their traditional use carried straight on. In 1805 yokes were still commonest in Herefordshire, though harness was on its way in. Similarly on the hilly ground of North Devon yokes were still preferred (Dickson 1805, 131). Even in Sussex collars were found alongside yokes by about the 1880s, when collars had become general in most other places where draught oxen survived. Collars of oat straw replaced the yoke and bow in the Isle of Man about 1812, allegedly because of shortage of wood in the island, but no doubt because it was the fashion of the times, and because oxen for the plough may have been innovations. Only plough horses were referred to in an earlier survey of 1794 (Quayle 1794, 19-20; Quayle 1812, 149-55; Killip 1966, 5). The early nineteenth-century Statistical Surveys tell the same story for Ireland.

The earliest use of collars on oxen in England has not been firmly ascertained, though an illustration from the Garleston Psalter (Anglian, 1310-1325) is said to show a team of four in a plough, with two horses before and two oxen behind, all apparently wearing collars. The artist's plough is so odd, however, that this evidence should not be too freely accepted. On the whole it is likely that the general adoption of collars does not antedate the improved plough types of the eighteenth century.

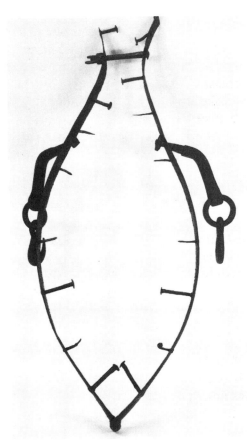

Fig. 8. The iron frame of an ox collar from Bures, Sussex. By permission of the Museum of English Rural Life, Neg. No. 60/609.

Ox collars are normally open at the top or bottom to allow them to be slipped over the animal's neck, and are completed by hames of wood or iron with hooks to take the trace ropes. A picture of Cirencester oxen in 1935 shows that the collars are open at the top. Dickson in the 1760s said the upper part of the collar was usually open (Dickson 1779, 257). In Aberdeenshire, Orkney, etc. (Fig. 6) they were usually open at the bottom, though not always, and no hard and fast regional distributions can be drawn. A special arrangement of apparently local provenance, from Bures in Suffolk, is illustrated in Fig. 8, where the iron frame of a collar (from which the padding has disappeared) was hinged at one end and closed by a nut and bolt at the other.

Conclusion

This study emphasises a number of factors. There is the contrast between the prehistoric horn yokes and, on the one hand, the teams of four horses abreast in the same area, and on the other, the universality of the bow yoke in Lowland Britain, in historic times. There is the relationship between the decline of oxen and the advance of agricultural improvement which can be matched elsewhere in Europe, for example in Poitou, where the change from the two to the three-course rotation coincided with the change from oxen to horses, about 1790. This must be further related to questions of cropping, for as Slicher van Bath has made clear, a low seed yield ratio means that a greater area must be cultivated to provide a required amount, so that a correspondingly greater number of animals has to be maintained (van Bath 1963, 22, 60-1). Thus the change from oxen to horses in Britain and elsewhere is intimately linked with improvements in land use and crop yields. It must also be related to factors like the development of hard roads, and the introduction of agricultural machinery such as, for example, the reaper, for which oxen would have been too slow. In Britain the revived use of oxen by improvers like the Duke of Queensberry in Wiltshire, Lord Clare in Essex, the Duke of Argyll in Western Scotland (Campbell 1774, 140; Cregeen 1964, 93, 144), and many others, does not, however, stem from war conditions, as in South Germany during the Thirty Years' War, when horses were plundered by the troops (van Bath 1963, 294), but seems rather to be (as in Sweden) a direct result of agrarian writing and theorising.

The subject is clearly one that can throw light on many aspects of the history of Britain, social, economic, and agrarian, and it remains to be studied in as close regional detail as it deserves.

Acknowledgements

Thanks are due to the many people who have helped with advice, illustrations, etc., in the preparation of this essay. I am particularly indebted to A. Jewell, Museum of English Rural Life; Dr A. T. Lucas, National Museum of Ireland; Dr A. Gailey, Ulster Folk Museum; the West Sussex County Record Office; J. N. Taylor, Gloucester Museum and Art Gallery; and the Manx Museum.

2

Early Yoke Types in Britain

In recent times, much fresh information has been published on yokes (Jacobeit and Kramařik 1968-69; Delamarre 1969) during the last 200 years. Several yokes of various forms have been found in Scotland and Ireland, mostly in peat bogs, but for earlier periods. None has been found so far in England. This essay brings together the data for the first time.

Most strikingly, no single one of these thirteen yokes parallels the withers yokes that alone are known in Britain from the medieval period until the nineteenth century A.D. Most of the withers yokes are double-bow yokes, and the ubiquity of this form, running well back into the Middle Ages, presents a striking contrast with the range of types from the earlier period. It is necessary to look at the early British yokes in a wide European context in order to interpret their significance, before attempting to pinpoint the period at which they were replaced by the double-bow withers yoke.

Previous writers on yokes have divided them into two broad groups, withers yokes and head or horn yokes. Generally speaking, head or horn yokes are fairly straight, with knobs or grooves to hold the thongs that pass round the horns. However, for earlier yoke types, it is not always easy to decide exactly which category they fall into.

Two of the Scottish yokes are undoubtedly head yokes (Fig. 9, 1-2). Fig. 9, 1, from Argyll in the West of Scotland, was found in 1890 (*Catalogue* 1892, 348). It has lightly curved neck-pieces, and a horizontal central opening that penetrates the base of a raised crest. The edges of the knobs and grooves for the retaining thongs are so sharp that it is possible to imagine that the yoke has never been in use. Its length is 104 cm.

Fig. 9, 2, found deep in a bog in the Shetland Islands, has three horizontal openings bored through a long comb. The two outer openings are set too far in from the neck-pieces to have served for the attachment of thongs to the horns, and may, therefore, have been intended to allow lateral adjustment of the beam or pole of a plough or vehicle. Its length is 140 cm.

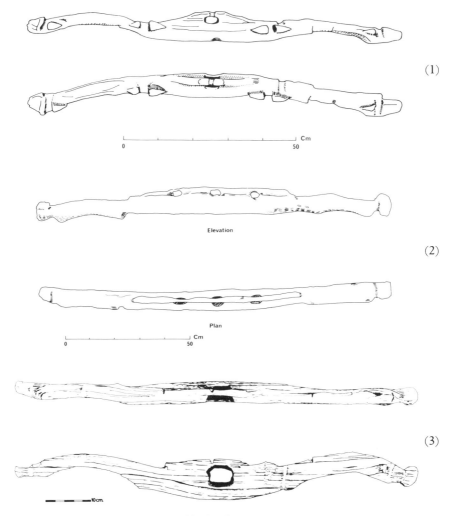

Fig. 9. Head yokes from 1. Argyll; 2. Shetland; 3. Baltigeer, Co. Meath, no. 1968:434.

A fairly close equivalent is the head-yoke from Baltigeer in County Meath, Ireland (Fig. 9, 3). It has a large, rectangular central opening, and a rather shallow comb. At the inner side of each neck-piece is a broad vertical groove where the horn thongs have been attached. Although it is a double yoke, it is only 86 cm. long.

Parallels to these three head yokes have been found in Denmark and in the Netherlands. The Danish examples (Fig. 10, 2-5) each have a single, horizontal, central opening at the base of a raised crest, and the yoke from Ezinge (Fig. 10, 1) in Holland has two angular grooves cut

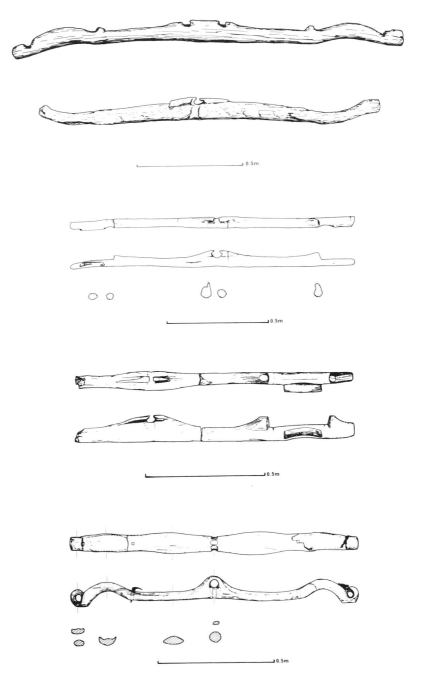

Fig. 10. A yoke from Ezinge. From a photograph, not to scale; 2. From Finderup; 3. Sevel; 4. Dejbjerg, 5. Lundgårdshede. No. 1 from Holland, all others from Denmark.

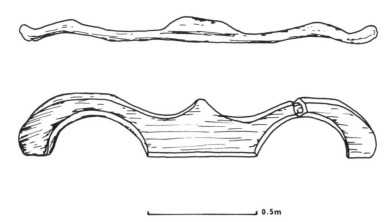

0.5m

Fig. 11. Yokes from 1. Vinelz, Switzerland After Gandert 1964; 2. Petersfehn, Oldenberg. After Hayen 1983.

in the crest. The Finderup yoke also has two vertical openings, one bored through each of the outermost ends, and the Dejbjerg yoke has two small horizontal openings, one on each of the inner sides of the neck-pieces. Thus, they do not parallel the British yokes exactly, though direct comparison is impossible when the precise working contexts are unknown. They are also bigger than the British yokes, that from Ezinge measuring 146 cm., and the Danish ones ranging up to 180 cm. in length.

Head yokes must have a considerable antiquity, and in this respect a comparable yoke-type found at Vinelz (Fig. 11, 1) in Switzerland (Gandert 1964, 37-8) should be looked at. According to O.-F. Gandert, this yoke, found in a lake-dwelling, can be dated to 2000 B.C. Though it is perhaps not easy to accept this early date too freely, nevertheless it is likely that head or horn yokes were amongst the earliest auxiliary devices used to adapt animals for draught purposes.

Generally speaking, it is probable that withers yokes are somewhat later in date, as has been shown for Finland (Vilkuna 1936, 2). Withers yokes normally have vertical openings placed at each side of the neck-pieces to take the upright pins and thongs that encircled the necks of the animals. Withers yokes from the Middle Ages onwards can be easily identified by these features, but unfortunately it is not so easy to categorise earlier specimens, some of which combine features of both head and withers yokes. Possibly some are hybrid forms due to the survival of features of the head yoke in withers yokes. Variations must also be due to the physiological differences between oxen and horses.

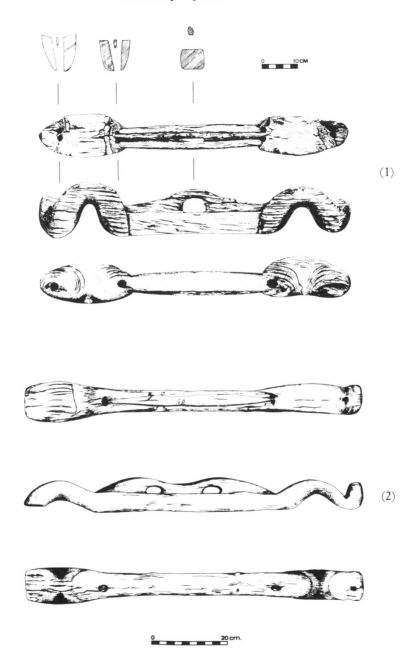

(1)

(2)

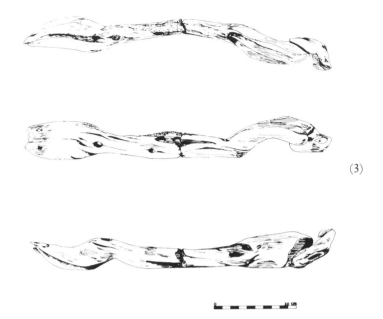

Fig. 12. Withers yokes from Ireland, 1. Toberdoney, Co. Antrim, no. R·2474 (Wk 299); 2. Florencecourt bog, Co. Fermanagh, no. R 2559 (Wk 300); 3. between Lisbellaw and Enniskillen, no. 1878:18 (Wk 302).

We still have to learn how these differences should be interpreted in terms of yoke forms. Gandert believed that a withers yoke (Fig. 11, 2), 169 cm. long, found in a moor at Petersfehn in Oldenberg, is as old as 2000-1700 B.C. (Gandert 1964, 38-42). This date is based on pollen-analysis of neighbouring peat. The yoke, however, bears marks of metal tools, and is much later. It has subsequently been radio-carbon dated to the 3rd-4th century A.D. (Hayen 1983, 20-21). One can feel on surer ground, however, with the dating of the yokes from wagon-graves found in South Russia and the Caucasus (Piggott 1969), from the 14th-13th centuries B.C. At all events, the possibility has to be kept open, that in at least certain areas, withers yokes are almost as early as head or horn yokes.

With these thoughts in mind, the remaining British yokes can now be examined. Three from Ireland (Fig. 12, 1-3) appear to be undoubted withers yokes. They are quite short (1: 84 cm.; 2: 84 cm.; 3: 87 cm.), shorter than the majority of withers yokes, but not much shorter than the metre-long neck yokes from Finland (Vilkuna 1936, 2). Like the head or horn yokes, they have each a central crest, and one or two central, horizontal openings to hold the lashings for a beam or pole.

The Fermanagh yoke (Fig. 12, 2) has a double crest. The neck-pieces are deep and well carved, with a vertical opening at each side. The inner openings, less often the outer ones, are catapult-shaped, i.e. they start as a single opening in the underside of the yoke beam, and split into two openings halfway up.

The yoke from Enniskillen (Fig. 12, 3) and another from Mayo (Fig. 16, 1) each have two lateral, V-shaped hollows above the neck-pieces, the result being the creation of three ridges. When looked at from above, the appearance, with the double openings that come out one on either side of the centre ridge, is remarkably like that of a snake's head. Parallels to these three-ridged neck-pieces can be found in the La-Tène period, *c.* 450 B.C. to the birth of Christ, and earlier in the Hallstatt period, late seventh-early sixth centuries B.C. Particular reference may be made to the two leather-covered and bronze-studded yokes found at Hradenín, near Kolín, and at Lovosice, in Bohemia (Filip 1962, 31-2; Piggott 1965, Pl. XXXIII; Drack 1958, 12-17). This group of Irish yokes, therefore, have clear La Tène and Hallstatt period analogies. The same form is also found in Denmark, for example for the yoke from Lundgårdshede in Jutland (Bro-Jorgensen 1966, 116-18). Instead of a crest, however, there is a peak, and the outer terminals have horizontal openings into which run vertical openings bored from above. The inner sides of the neck-pieces have vertical openings only. Fragments of leather thongs were found in these openings (Fig. 10, 5). This yoke is possibly the only one to have been radio-carbon dated. According to the calculations of the Radio-Carbon Laboratory in Copenhagen, it must be attributed to 330 B.C. (Lerche 1968, 59-60). It will be important for future investigations of early forms of transport and draught to establish the dates of a further selection of yoke types by the radio-carbon method, especially those found in peat bogs and not stratified or associated with other datable finds.

Two of the other Irish yokes have horizontal openings in their outer terminals. The first (Fig. 13, 1) appears to be unparalleled in form. The surviving outer opening takes the form of a vertical slit, matched on the inner side of the neck-piece by a groove in which the wear-marks of the thongs are readily visible. Seen from above, the neck-pieces are not symmetrical, each having a flap at one side. This is almost certainly a head yoke, that had been fastened by thongs to the inner horns, and by straps, if the vertical slot is any criterion, to the outer horns.

The second yoke (Fig. 13, 2) in this category is the well-known one from Dungannon in Northern Ireland (Piggott 1949, 192-3; Jacobeit

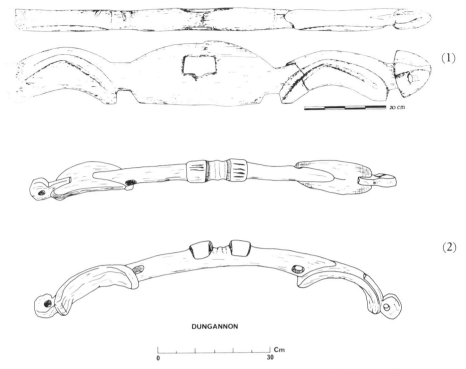

Fig. 13. Irish yokes with horizontal openings in the outer terminals, from 1. Cloontooa, Co. Galway, no. 1945:175; 2. Dungannon.

1953, 95-7). In this case there are circular, horizontal openings at either side of the neck-pieces. This yoke, as a whole, is extremely well-shaped and has distinct analogies with yokes of the La-Tène and Hallstatt periods. The broad neck-pieces protrude symmetrically front and back, which is unusual for a head yoke, and the question of whether or not this is a yoke for a pair of horses must remain open.

Next comes a group of four yokes, three from Ireland (Fig. 14, 1-3), and one from Scotland (Fig. 16, 7). The latter is shaped, but has no openings cut in it and is, therefore, not ready for use. All four have deep, narrow neck-pieces. The Irish examples each have an oval opening for the beam or pole lashings, horizontal openings on the inner sides of the neck-pieces, and vertical openings in the outer terminals. In the long ridge above the neck-pieces or just to one side there is a further pair of horizontal openings, which may be explained by comparison with the Swedish withers yokes that have openings or attachment points at these positions for extra ropes or thongs going

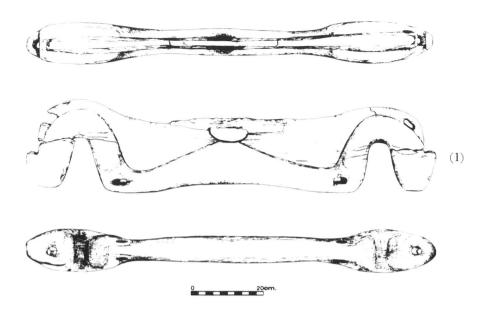

0 20 om.

(1)

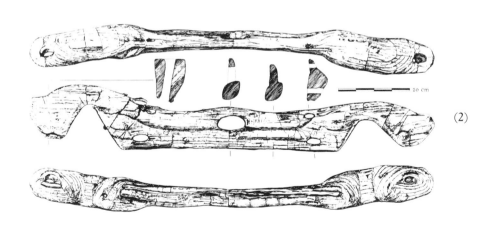

20 cm

(2)

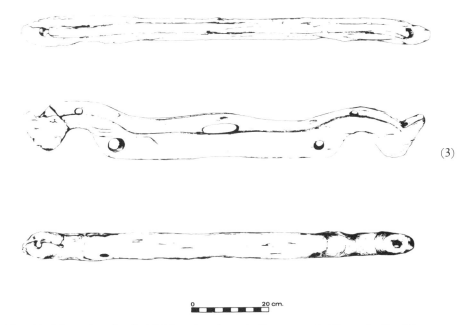

(3)

0 ━━━━━━ 20 cm.

Fig. 14. Three deep-bodied Irish yokes from 1. Carrowreagh (Cooper), Co. Sligo, no. 1968:441; 2. Donagh, Co. Monaghan, no. Wk 142; 3. Co. Meath, no. R 1901 (Wk 301).

round the horns. If this is so, then this group of four yokes was intended for ox-draught. All are deep and heavy, and measure from 110-120 cm. in length.

Finally, there is a yoke from Mayo in Ireland, one end of which has been broken off. It can be established from the remaining part, however, that it originally measured 213 cm. long, i.e. about twice as long as any other early British yokes (Fig. 15). Its later parallels in Shetland and Wales are discussed above. There is plenty of evidence to suggest that the Irish yoke was also used with a team of four oxen, and it is further of interest to note that the three-ridged neck-piece has analogies in the La Tène and Hallstatt periods. Even if the yoke is not quite as early as that, it must still be early, and with it, possibly, the method of arranging a draught team four abreast. This withers yoke has vertical openings in the outer terminals, and a small hole above the neck-piece to which a horn-thong was no doubt attached.

The catalogue of Irish and Scottish yoke types raises many problems relating to form and function that can only be resolved by further investigation of a comparative nature. It is clear, however, that the

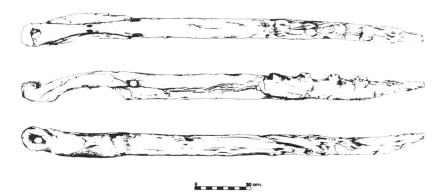

Fig. 15. Part of a very long Irish yoke, from Erriff Bog, near Ballyhaunis, Co. Mayo, no. 1909:52.

question of draught is an important and essential element that must be considered as part of any study of the early history of transport or cultivation.

Footnote. Since this essay was first written, a number of other yokes have been pinpointed, six in Ireland, and one in Scotland.

Fig. 16, 1 is comparable to Fig. 12, 1. Fig. 16, 2, though badly twisted, has neck pads that equate it with Fig. 13, 2. Fig. 16, 3-4 are fragmentary, but are clearly parts of yokes. These are in the National Museum of Ireland.

The Armagh County Museum contains two examples. Fig. 16, 5 is a finely made yoke, crisply shaped, with two neck pads. Its closest parallel in this group is the Argyll yoke, Fig. 9, 1. Less well-made, and seemingly unfinished, is Fig. 16, 6.

The additional Scottish yoke, Fig. 16, 7, is likewise unfinished. It has been shaped, but no openings have been made in it. In the depth of its body it matches Fig. 14, 2 and 3.

This is, therefore, not only a surprising range of forms, but also a set of comparisons between the yokes of Ireland and of Scotland, or at least Argyll, which point to a close similarity in cultural traditions.

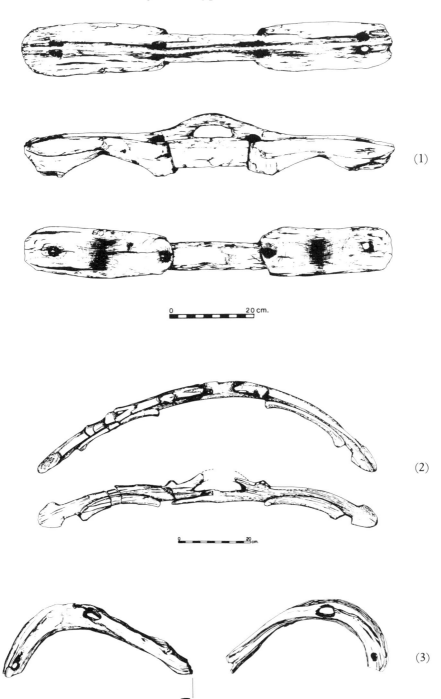

(1)

(2)

(3)

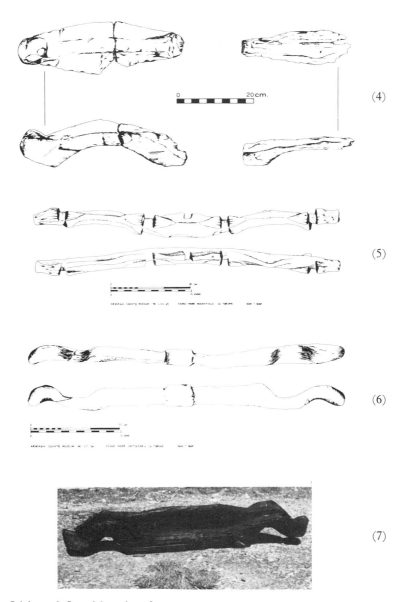

Fig. 16. Irish and Scottish yokes from 1. Donagh, Co. Monaghan, no. 1955:4; 2. Carrowntryla, Co. Galway, no. 1969:730; 3. Cloonascragh, Co. Galway, no. 1932:6496, A. B; 4. Loughduff Bog, Derrykinlough, Co. Mayo, nos. 1954:8 and 1954:15; 5. near Mountfield, Co. Tyrone, no. L103-69; 6. near Castlederg, Co. Tyrone, no. 127-56; 7. a roughly shaped but incomplete yoke from Islay, Scotland, 40 in. long by 8 in. deep. Nos. 9,1 and 13,2 in the National Museum of Antiquities of Scotland; nos. 16,5-6 in the Armagh County Museum; all others in the National Museum of Ireland. No. 16,7 was photographed by Miss K. M. Dickie, FSA Scot.

Part II

Turf and Seaweed Manure

3

Seaweed Manure

In a study of regional ethnology, it is important to consider the available resources, to examine how these are òr have been exploited, and to consider what control factors have been used to permit a reasonable distribution of the resource, and to prevent its over-exploitation. One such resource is seaweed, one of the most readily available forms of manure around the coasts of Scotland, where it has probably been in use as a fertiliser as long as agriculture in any organised form has existed. Scotland probably has a greater quantity of seaweed growing round her shores than most countries. In the littoral zone between high and low water mark, a survey carried out in the 1940s gave a figure of 180,000 tons. The distribution showed that 70% of the total quantity available was concentrated on the Outer Hebrides:

Area	Tons	Acres	Tons per Acre
Outer Hebrides	125,136	3,500	36
Inner Hebrides	8,263	278	30
Orkney	38,774	1,813	21
Mainland, W. and NW.	8,540	356	24

In the sub-littoral zone, the resources are enormous, extending to over 1,000,000 tons in Orkney waters alone (Jackson 1948, 137, 142). Neither at present, nor in the past, has seaweed been scarce.

Though it still serves to manure the ground in some areas, it has largely been replaced by the readily available commercial types of fertiliser, which are far easier to handle and less demanding in terms of manpower. Nevertheless its past history in the different regions of Scotland is an important pointer to the community life and organisations of these areas.

As a food for plants, seaweed is of value to any soil. It is rich in potassium, and also provides nitrogen and organic matter. It is equivalent to farmyard manure in nitrogen content, and contains roughly twice the amount of potassium. Seaweed is particularly good for sandy soils, since these tend to be deficient in potassium, and its gelatinous nature improves the soil's water-holding capacity. The oarweeds and wracks are particularly good for potatoes, though the salt content may produce a waxiness in the tubers which can be counteracted by ploughing in the seaweed in late autumn, or by making it into a compost. On the negative side, seaweed is, as a rule, deficient in lime and in phosphates, having only about a third of the phosphorus content of farmyard manure.

Curiously enough, therefore, one eighteenth-century agricultural writer thought it 'very proper for land that is exhausted by lime or ashes' (Dickson 1770, I. 430). Too long continued use of seaweed alone can be bad for the soil because of this imbalance in its chemical content (Darling 1945, 27; Darling 1955, 213-4; Dickinson 1963, 29-30). For this reason it was often used along with other kinds of manure, often in the form of composts.

Seaweeds of the *Corallinaceae* family, such as the species of *Lithothamnion* found all along the west coasts, could also be of benefit, since the broken fragments, washed up in the form of lime-rich sand, make a good dressing for acid soils (Dickinson 1963, 29-30). This, however, is an indirect form of use.

The effect of seaweed is said not to be as lasting as that of farmyard dung, which necessitated applying fresh seaweed each year but nevertheless, 'the value of seaweed, when it can be procured from the neighbourhood, can hardly be sufficiently estimated, as it has not only a wonderful effect in enriching light soils, but of making them produce more grain than even the appearance of the crop would warrant. Seaweed also acts as a condiment; for both cattle and sheep not only eat with avidity the grass on which it is spread, but thrive faster, and are sooner fattened, than on grounds to which it is not applied' (Sinclair II (1814), 528).

Except for clay soils in wet weather, or land recently laid down with grass and clover seed, seaweed was of general value. There were different theories about the best method of application, however. The saying, 'better unled than unspread', supported the view that it should be spread fresh, straight from the cart. Some thought its good effects would be lost if it were put into heaps (Sinclair II (1814), 528), though it was put into heaps in many places. It was suggested, presumably as a compromise, that if heaped, the heaps should be covered with mould (Naismith 1814, 79), but this was certainly not the practice in the islands of the North and West, except insofar as composting it in layers with other manures had an equivalent effect. Where seaweed was plentiful, both methods were used. What was washed ashore in spring was spread fresh, and what was washed up in winter was built into middens for later use.

The composting of seaweed was a practice developed empirically long before the days of the agricultural writers. Naismith, for example, recommended mixing it with peat-moss, since fermentation then started easily (this phenomenon was widely known). He also favoured laying a thick layer of seaweed in the dung-stead and covering it immediately with a thick layer of farmyard dung (Naismith 1814, 79-80).

Another advantage of seaweed manure was that it was unfavourable to weeds (Dickson 1770, 431).

As may be seen from the details in the regional survey that follows, seaweed was an immensely valuable resource. To get it, people were prepared to argue, to fight, and to break the Sabbath. Where it was available, the rent of the land was often higher. It is, perhaps, astonishing in the light of past history, that this excellent manure is now so little used.

Types, Terminology and Habitat

The seaweed types primarily used for manure are the Laminareae and Fucaceae. The former includes *Laminaria*, oarweed, *Laminaria digitata*, tangle, and *L. saccharina*, sea belt. The latter are the wracks, and include *Fucus vesiculosus*, bladderwrack, *Ascophyllum nodosus*, knotted wrack, and *Pelvetia caniculata*, channelled wrack (Dickinson 1963, 82 ff.). Earlier writers usually pinpoint four main species used in manuring. These were named, for example, *Fucus vesiculosus*, *F. nodosus*, *F. digitatus* and *F. serratus*, the latter being most common at the heads of narrow bays and the upper parts of river mouths, but said to have the weakest effect of the four (Naismith 1814, 79). A later writer named the same group as *Laminaria saccharina*, *L. digitata*, *Fucus vesiculosus*, and *Halidrys siliquosa*, the two latter having air bladders (Stephens II (1844), 415).

Apart from these botanical names, which had not yet quite settled down in the scientific writings, there were several dialect names that distinguished different qualities and kinds of seaweed, both in Gaelic and in the Scottish dialects. These will not be discussed in detail here, however, the chief point of importance being that the standard Scottish names, *ware*, and *tang* or *tangle*, make a broad distinction in habitat, summed up by the statement that 'Tang grows upon the Rocks above the Low-water Mark, and Wair grows in the Sea, without the Low-water Mark' (*Session Papers* 6 July 1759, 41).

As will appear, these differences in habitat reflect differences in the times and methods of collection, and also in the uses to which the seaweed was put, whether for manure or for kelp making.

South-East Scotland

Though the main seaweed areas of Scotland lie in the North and West, this resource was just as highly valued, earlier on, in the farming districts of the South-East. The first recorded reference for Scotland as a whole relates to an island in the Firth of Forth, 'insulam et rupem de Inchgarde — cum mettagiis, ancoragiis, *le wrak* et *le ware*' (*Reg. Mag. Sig. Scot.* 1882, 429). Possibly the two terms, if not an alliterative couplet, may indicate a distinction between washed up and growing seaweed.

In 1636, it was in use around Dunbar and North Berwick (Brown 1891, 135), and still in the 1790s in Dirleton (*OSA* III (1792), 195) and Dunbar (*OSA* V (1793), 455). It was also keeping up the price of land in Innerwick parish (*OSA* I (1791), 122), and indeed the rents of coastal farms were 25/- — 30/- an acre more than those inland (Kerr 1809, 377). Not all farmers valued it equally, however, for though much used by some, it was neglected by others, especially in the neighbouring county of Berwickshire (Home 1797, 95).

The kind of seaweed was sub-littoral tangle, with a long stalk and broad spreading leaf. It extended over half a mile off Cockburnspath, according to the fishermen, and lay up to 20 fathoms deep, 'like a forest', growing to a height of 8-10 feet. Where washed up by storms, it was eagerly gathered, spread, and ploughed in as fresh as possible (*OSA* XIII (1794), 224-5).

Some farmers had roads made at great expense to go down steep crags for seaweed, some suitable for carts, others practicable only for horses harnessed with panniers, baskets, or creels whose bottoms could be opened by pulling out a peg (Kerr 1809, 374-5). After a spring tide or a storm, all other work ceased in order to save the seaweed before it was carried away.

Here it was thought best to spread the seaweed fresh, because of the quick solubility of the 'gluten' it contained. If left in a heap, this would be washed out. It went on to whatever part of the farm required manure, for crops of any kind, and was also used to force a large second (or even a third) cutting by being laid on newly cut clover. It was particularly good for light soils, less so for clay (Somerville 1805, 184). When composted with 'long litter' or any available vegetable rubbish, it helped to promote putrefaction (Kerr 1809, 376-7).

The rate of application was 25-40 cartloads per acre (Kerr 1809, 377). In the mid-nineteenth century many East Lothian farms manured 100-120 imperial acres a year with seaweed at a rate of 30 double cart-loads per acre — i.e. 3000-3600 cartloads per season (Stephens III (1844), 1238), which gives some indication of the labour-intensive nature of seaweed manuring. A cartload of good seaweed was con-sidered as good as a cartload of dung, and more so at barley-sowing time when it was at its ripest (*OSA* XIII (1794), 225).

As in most parts of Scotland, seaweed manure was applied especially to the barley crop. As a result, there was on Lowland coastal farms a type known as *ware barley* (Buchan-Hepburn 1794, 75), sometimes said to be inferior in quality and appearance (Wight IV (1783), 479). Nevertheless, ware-barley was preferred by brewers on account of its fairer colour and thinner husk (*OSA* XIII (1794), 225; Forsyth IV (1806), 522) and was in demand for seed, especially by upland farmers. It was said to ripen a week earlier than the other barley types, and fetched 1/- more per boll (*OSA* XIII (1794), 225).

Seaweed manure was in active, though increasingly sporadic, use in this area till well through the nineteenth century (Stephens III (1844), 1238; II (1845), 309; Johnston 1853, 286).

East Scotland: Fife and Angus

In this area the inhabitants of the towns and burghs on the coast were as much interested in seaweed as the country farmers, a fact that highlights the contemporary closeness of the links between country and town, for a good proportion of the inhabitants of towns and burghs had land which they farmed. The availability of town manure may, in fact, have meant that their returns were better than those of their purely rural contemporaries. However, they also valued seaweed highly. There are recurrent statutes about the division of sea ware in the burgh of Crail in the county of Fife. The rights of the inhabitants to the ware were defended against those of others dwelling outside the burgh. On 14 November 1570, it was emphasised that the inhabitants should be allowed to transport and lead away whatever ware was cast ashore within the burgh boundaries, 'according to thair awld privilege use and possesion obseruit vsit past memoir of man'. On 6 October 1572, it was 'statute and ordinate — that na vther persoun duelland owtwith the burrow ruidis off the said brugh collect gadder transporte or cary away ony wair or fuilyie fra the sea cost' within the burgh limits and privileges without the permission of the bailies and council.

A further kind of control was aimed at conserving this valuable resource. On 3 November 1590, it was ordained that no one in the burgh should gather ware at any time before 7 o'clock in the morning, 'nor that thei pas or waide within the vater For gaddering thairoff, forther nor thei mey stand vpon the dry land and draw the samyn to land with thair cleik, And that na wair be keipit togidder or putt in middingis within this burgh or owtwith the samyn narrer the sea nor the eist grene or wind mylne wnder the pane of aucht s. vnlaw (fine)' (Murray 1964, 90-91). Thus both the method of collection, and the places where the ware might be heaped up in middens, were defined.

In spite of repeated regulations, there was constant bickering. In 1663, near Culross and Torryburn further up the Firth of Forth, James Carmichaell, brother german to Sir David Carmichaell of Balmedy, was 'overseeing some of his servants lading their carts with sea-ware for manuring the ground, as has been their custom for years past'. As they were doing so, John Mercer, officer at Culross, and others, came with staves and clubs and unyoked the horses, seized the forks, forced the carters to empty their loads, and drove the others away. This was done because several acts aimed at protecting his seaweed had been made in the burgh court of Torryburn by Lord Colvill, who owned the shore rights with 'the benefit of cutting, shearing and ingathering the ware thereof' (*Reg. P.C. Scot.* I (1908), 386-7). From this it appears that, in addition to the collection by means of iron cleeks or hooks mentioned at Crail, cutting of the weed was also done. Transport here was on a fairly large scale in carts drawn by horses. 'Slaids' or sledges are mentioned in the same source.

In the country areas rights of ownership and access were just as eagerly maintained. In 1499-1500, an action was taken by David Lindesay of Montago and his brother Walter, against Thomas Maule, for preventing them and their tenants in the 'toune and landis of Skryne' in Angus from taking the seaware and laying it on these lands as manure, 'as was usit and wont in times bigane' (*Act. Dom. Conc.* II (1918), 350). On 15 October 1528, an obligation is recorded by

Alexander Myrtone, laird of Randelston, to Sir William Myrtone, vicar of the parish church of Lawthrysk, of five acres of Randelston, with grazing for a horse, and free access to and from the ware with as many horses as needed for the cultivation of his five acres (Rogers 1877, 374).

An account of Angus written about 1682 stated that there was an abundance of sea ware along the coast, 'which occasions a great increase of cornes where it is laid' (Ochterlony I (1844), 320), and in 1733 the magistrate and council of Arbroath were trying to control this resource by making all those who gathered it lead it to the east of a particular ditch (*Arbroath T. C. Minutes MS* (24 October) 1733, 178).

However, it is not until the 1790s that information about theory and practice, as opposed to legal squabbles, becomes available.

When cast up by high tides and storms, it was spread straight away, rather than left in heaps. In Fife, it was thought better to leave it spread on the surface, whether as a top-dressing for grass, or some other crop, rather than to plough it down, on the grounds that when spread and exposed to the air it soon dissolved and mixed with the soil (Thomson 1800, 247). In Angus, manuring with *red-ware* or *tangle* was chiefly for barley, at a rate of 50 cartloads per Scots acre (1.26 imperial acres). Gathering of seaweed was normally done in spring, when it was needed. Heaping into middens or composting does not appear to have been common (Headrick 1813, 416). According to Stephens, the Fife folk thought 16 loads of seaware equivalent to 20 loads of farmyard dung. The cost of transport was reckoned at 1/- — 1/2 per cartload, and on the east coast of Fife, the availability of sea ware put up the price of land by as much as 10/- an acre. It is little wonder, therefore, that all hands were set to work if there was a risk of losing a bank of seaweed (Stephens III (1844), 1238).

Seaweed manuring was recorded in the 1790s in Fife for the parishes of Anstruther Wester (*OSA* III (1792), 78), Burntisland (*OSA* II (1792), 428), Kilrenny (*OSA* I (1791), 410) and in Angus for Arbirlot (*OSA* III (1792), 468) and Panbride (*OSA* I (1791), 439).

By the mid-nineteenth century, however, seaweed manuring was on the wane, not only because in places like the parish of Kingsbarns in Fife less had come ashore in recent years than formerly (*NSA* IX (1845), 90), but also because of the trouble and expense involved in collection (*NSA* IX (1845), 156: Abbotshall). Lowland farming, in fact, was moving more and more into a kind of money-based economy, in which manpower had to be paid for.

The North-East: (a) Kincardine, Aberdeen, Banff, Nairn and Moray

In the mid-seventeenth century, the people of Banff were so eager to gather seaweed that they were prepared to profane the Lord's day by starting at 8 or 10 o'clock on Sunday night. They were therefore forbidden to gather ware 'efter seting of the sone on Saturday till Monday that the sone be risen again' (Cramond I (1891), 139). Similar complaints about Sabbath breaking were being made in Aberdour in 1699 (Cramond 1896, 42).

In Aberdeenshire, ware bere began to be referred to in the official price lists in 1655, and a fiars price continued to be struck for it until 1808. This special treatment shows how general a practice seaweed-manuring was (*Misc. N. S. C.* II (1908), 10). Ware bere was here thought inferior to other kinds (Anderson 1794, 109), and was given a slightly lower price (*Ib*; *Caled. Mag.* 21 March 1783, 64). This may in part have been because the grain was very small, even though the crop was abundant. In terms of comparative weights (Amsterdam weight and Aberdeen measure), ware bere ran at 16-17 stone to the boll, common country bere at 17-18 stone to the boll, and true barley at 19-20 stone to the boll (*OSA* VI (1793), 17: Rathen). Curiously, however, on the heavy clays of East Lothian (as opposed to the light loams and gravelly soils of north-east Scotland), ware bere was said to be always of the best quality (Keith 1811, 434), though as previously noted this was not a universally held view.

An interesting point relating to economics comes from Nairn and Moray, where it was thought that seaweed manuring benefited the proprietor more than the tenant, since the greater quantity of grain produced allowed him to increase the rents, without regard for the expense of collection and transport that the tenant had to bear (Leslie 1811, 283).

In about 1662, Gordon of Straloch wrote a description of Enzie ('Ainia') in Banffshire, which stated (betraying a lack of knowledge of the fact that seaweed was not a substitute for lime): 'Hic, deficiente calce, agri oceano vicini alga marina stercorantur, cujus vis magna, accedente bis quotidiano aestu, in littus ejicitur: adsunt servi observatis horis, et, ne quid pereat, recedente aestu algam fugientem retrahunt, sese undis, saeva hyeme (etiam saepe noctu), immergentes. Caeterum, haec agriculturae ratio non his locis propria sed quam late patent littora, et mare propinquum, omnibus communis, nisi scopuli prohibeant' (*Collections* 1843, 13).

Thus the workers who gathered seaweed were at the beck and call of the sea not only after the east and north winds had driven ware ashore (Macfarlane (1721) I (1906), 45-6), but also at every tide. It is not surprising, therefore, that farm servants on the coast had better pay than those inland, because of this heavy involvement with ware. The Regulations of Fees for the Servants in the county of Banff, for 1760, stated:

	£. s. d.
That the best man servant who drags the ware, and is capable to big (build) and sow corns, shall have	27 0 0
That the second man servant who fills the side of the ware horse, threshes the side of the barn, lays on loads, and is a good hook (shearer) at harvest, shall have	25 0 0
That the third man who likewise fills the ware horse, is capable to thresh the side of the barn, and can shear in harvest, shall have	20 0 0.

These wages compared with £23, £19.4.0 and £13.6.8 for similar servants in areas without seaweed. The higher wages are a clear indication of the extra hard work involved in the gathering and transport of seaweed, in this case in panniers on horseback, and perhaps they also indicate better returns (Dunbar 1865, 97).

As usual, detail is considerably expanded by the later sources. It appears, for example, that the reason why there seem to be few early references for Kincardine is that the thirty-mile coast of this county is for the most part too precipitous for ware, apart from a few recesses between Bervie and the mouth of the River North Esk, where small quantities, not exceeding 3000 cartloads in a season, were lodged from time to time (Robertson 1813, 375). Nigg Bay, just south of Aberdeen, got a supply when an offshore wind caused an undercurrent that brought the seaweed to the land. It produced bere of a slightly inferior quality (*OSA* VII (1793), 201-2).

In the Banffshire parish of Gamrie, seaware was laid on sparingly for a barley crop due to the steepness of the cliffs and the bad access (*OSA* I (1791), 471), but plenty was available for the work of getting it. When winds drove it ashore, 'no work is suffered to interrupt the pursuit of it' and it might be transported for distances up to two or three miles (*OSA* XIV (1795), 266: Bellie). Men, women and horses might be employed day and night until all had been secured (Leslie 1811, 283). The species called 'belly-weed' (the 'babby-ware' referred to in the Peterhead parish account, *OSA* XVI (1795), 552, is probably a misprint for this), i.e. *bell-ware* or *Fucus vesiculosus*, was also cut for manure (*OSA* III (1792), 47).

The value of seaware may be gauged from the fact that a three-quarter acre field on a Banffshire estate had grown good crops of barley mainly by this means for 47 years without a break (*OSA* XIII (1794), 395: Rathven). The system of management in the 1790s, at least in parts of the area, was to spread 300 cartloads per acre on ley in summer, another 160 cartloads after the crop had been cut all night during the winter, and another 100 loads in April-May when the seaweed was at its strongest for manure. This enormous task, however, was undertaken only every second year in Rathven parish (*Ib.*, 396). This appears to be a development on the situation in 1683, when 400 loads per acre were applied to bere (*Collections* 1843, 102). Besides direct spreading, composting of sea tang with earth was also practised (Pennant 1776, 150).

Little direct evidence for the regulation of the seaweed shores has been noted for the area, but no doubt rights were as jealously guarded as elsewhere. People who had relatively little seaware would have to pay for permission to gather it elsewhere, like the tenants of Rattray (*Abd. Jnl.* (10 October) 1794), and the privilege of 'Wairing and Wairgate' (i.e. access to the ware) was confirmed for the shores of Cairnbulg and Cairnglass as recently as 1849 (*Private Acts* 1849 c. 14). This alliterative terminology has a ring of antiquity but, in general, it may be that the apparent lack of early information on this aspect reflects a situation where abundance of seaweed made squabbling over it hardly necessary.

A further suggestion of the antiquity of seaweed manuring here stems from the fact that this is one of the few mainland regions where a custom is associated with seaweed gathering. The farmers on the sea-coast went to the shore on the early morning of the New Year for a 'draucht (load) o' waar', and seem to have vied with each other in getting the first load. No other work was done on that day (Gregor MSS. *c.* 1880). When the first load was carted home, a small quantity was laid down at each door in the steading, and the rest was put into the fields, a portion going into each. This was said to bring good fortune. The practice was recorded in the 1880s from someone who had followed it (Gregor II (1884), 331).

With the early nineteenth century, a change in emphasis occurred (as generally in the coastal parts of Lowland Scotland). Where previously ware had been applied to the bere crop, now it began to be used more for turnips, then of recent introduction as a field crop. Since this development took place at a time when artificial fertilisers, bone dust, guano, etc. were coming into ever more frequent use, it hastened the end of the extensive application of seaware as one of the primary manures for barley.

The North-East: (b) Ross and Cromarty, Inverness, Sutherland and Caithness

Only a little seaware was available on the short seaboard of the east side of Inverness. It was used in the parish of Inverness, along with street dung (*OSA* IX (1793), 612), and in Petty, where it was thought good for barley in strong land, but not so good for light soils which it opened up too much in dry weather (*OSA* III (1792), 27).

Further north, in Ross, seaweed was applied on the Fowlis estate, along with lime from Portsoy in Banffshire (Wight V/1 (1784), 239-240), the one undoubtedly supplementing the other in this area of improved farming. Seaweed also served the farmers of Fearn (*OSA* III (1792), 290) and in the mid-nineteenth century, Rosemarkie farmers either spread it fresh, or composted it. The latter was thought preferable (*NSA* XIV (1845), 355). In Nigg, seaware was applied as well as lime and bone-manure (*NSA* (1836), 34).

In Sutherland, seaweed was plentiful around Dunrobin, where all hands helped to secure it in winter. It could be composted with earth for the bere crop, but as a rule was spread, and ploughed in when dry. It was thought best for light ground. In December and January, it was spread on grass, laid so thickly that not a blade was to be seen (Wight V/I (1784), 300). It was also used in Golspie (*OSA* XXI (1799), 216), and in Clyne (*OSA* X (1794), 300).

At Embo in Dornoch, a public meeting was held to decide the collecting date for seaweed, which was known by the Gaelic name of *straileach*. This was pulled off the rocks in March and carried to the field in wicker baskets, *sgul*, shaped like half a mussel shell (Mackay n.d., 42).

In Caithness, in the extreme north-east tip of Scotland, a rugged coastline limited seaweed collection to certain places, but where it could be got it was intensively applied. Thus in 1699 the cottars on the estate of Mey were assembled, and from 11-26 December inclusive they were occupied in manuring the land with ware for the spring sowing. It is suggested that there were 50 or 60 of them, but even so their rate of progress was not fast enough to please the laird, who organised the work (Donaldson 1938, 122, 126).

In the 1790s, tang or seaware was the main manure in the parish of

Canisbay, specially abundant in spring. It was said that 'a wind blowing from the land brings the ware from the sea'. It cleaned the soil, and its constant use had made the soil of the parish as 'fine and friable as garden mould', and easy to cultivate. Dunghills of mixed earth and seaware, left to stand for 6-12 months, were favoured (*OSA* VIII (1792), 147). In Wick, the seaweed dunghills had an intermixture of cod's heads, herring garbage, and brine (*OSA* X (1794), 7). Seaware was also got in Reay (*OSA* VII (1793), 275).

As well as composts, fresh seaweed was also widely collected, spread, and ploughed in immediately. The commonest kind, called *Alga fucus marinus* or 'great-tangle-weed', shrank on the dunghills from six cart-loads to less than one. 'Bell ware' or *Zostera marina*, the kelp weed, was also common. It was said not to shrink in the dunghill, and to be a better manure than the great tangle (Henderson 1812, 182).

About the turn of the century, some experimentation was taking place in the making of dunghills composted of seaweed and peat-earth, on a system to which the name of Lord Meadowbank was given. The method was thus: 'Make a layer of peat-moss, about 15 feet broad, eight feet long and six inches thick, then cover it with a layer or stratum of fresh sea-weed, six inches thick, and so on, stratum super stratum, until the heap is about five feet high, and tapering to a narrow ridge on the summit, like the roof of a house. The first cut being thus finished, commence another cut of six, seven, or eight feet long, at the end of it, and so on, piece after piece, as the weed and peat-moss can be collected, until the heap is of any convenient length and all of the same shape and height'. Dead moss earth should be used, and allowed to dry a little before being mixed in. It should be just moist enough to adhere together, when pressed in the hand, and should be cut up very small. The whole heap should be completely turned over in March or April, ready for application to the bere in May, or the turnips in June. The heap should not be pressed down, as this would prevent fermentation (Henderson 1812, 183-4).

In compiling his Agricultural Survey, Henderson was helped by a number of people whose reports are outlined in an Appendix. These show that ware was in regular use on the Earl of Caithness's farm of Mey, at Sandside (spread fresh), at Brabster (applied rotten), at Achingale and Keiss (composted with earth and stable dung), at Warse, Isauld and Thurso-East (compost of rotted seaware and dung), at Wester Ormly (composted in layers alternating with garden earth from the town of Thurso), at Spring Park (where the Meadowbank system was being tried, using dung rather than peatmoss), at East Noss (a sophisticated mixture of earth, shell-sand, seaware and summer dung, covered over during winter with winter dung, for turnips), and at Whitefield and Bleachfield (composted with earth). Most of the farmers on these places also spread seaware fresh in winter and spring, but one point made is that composts were more of a rule in areas where seaweed was scarce. In composting, one cartload of fresh seaweed was enough to reduce three cartloads of earth (Henderson 1812, Appx., 151-159).

Amongst these farmers, therefore, there were the two basic practices of spreading fresh and composting, depending partly on the time of year and partly on the accessibility of seaweed, and within each method a considerable amount of experiment and variation was possible.

The Northern Isles: Orkney and Shetland

Most of the inhabited parts of the Northern Isles are richly supplied with seaweed, and Orkney perhaps used more than any other part of Britain. The ware beaches were well-organised from early times, for even the earliest references reflect a much older tradition. Thus, at a court held in Orkney on 27 April 1509, it was decided that the farming community of Toab should not have the right of taking seaweed from the shore of Sabay (Johnston I (1907-13), 251-3). Ten years later, the matter was not resolved, for on 24 October 1519, a similar decision was taken — probably not for the first and not for the last time. This time, John Irvine of Sabay 'offerit to proof that he susteinet great wrang of the nychtbouris of Toep, in pasturing of thair guidis (live stock) on his ground . . . and sicklyk cam to his ground and bankis of Quhago, and tuik away his wair without leive or payment, as they war wont to pay for to him yeirlie'. The people in Toab agreed they had no rights to the ware, but said they had had leave to take it and had paid for it, as in the past. The exact boundaries between Toab and Sabay were then discussed and confirmed, and the court concluded: 'becaus it is notourlie knawin the ground and land of Quhaigo justlie appertenis to the airis (heirs) of Saba, and thairfor doome giwis that the nychtbouris of Thoep nor na wtheris sall tak nather aird nor stane nor wair nor ony wther thing af the ground of Saba, without leive askit and giwin, and gif thay do nocht, to pay a mark for everie laid or loading vnaskit leive or grantit thairto' (Johnston I (1907-13), 61-64).

A source allegedly dated 1592, which states that the Orkney people manured their land with seaware, and scorned midden manure (Ben in Macfarlane III (1908), 324) cannot be accepted, since the comment forms part of an English addition to the Latin text. The addition, on internal evidence, can scarcely be older than the eighteenth century.

In 1544, a piece of land was given 'cum privilegio lucrandi *lie wair* marium pro terris stercorandis' (*Reg. Mag. Sig. Scot.* 1883, 727/1). In 1627, a Report of the Commissioners for trying the Estate of the Paroch of Stennis noted that in the parts that lay far from the sea between hills, the land was so poor for lack of ware and manure, that it could not pay the duty imposed on it by his Majesty's chamberlain (Peterkin III (1820), 77). In the inland parish of Harray also, little seaweed was used in the seventeenth century, and it may be that the people there were exhibiting jealousy of their more fortunate neighbours when they suggested that ale made from bere fertilised by seaweed had a sharp taste (Mackaile in Barry 1805, 449).

Seaware was carried from the shore by means of horses, or on the human back, but not very far, for wet seaweed is heavy. For this reason, 'the skirts of the Isles are more ordinarily well cultivated, and do more abound with Corns, than places at a greater distance from the Sea, where they have not such gooding at hand' (Brand 1701, 19). When storms drove the ware ashore, 'all the people of the neighbour-hood come and divide the wrack according to the proportion of land they have about that place; but methinks, it is the greatest slavery in the world for the common people, as they do there in winter, to carry this wrack in small vessels made of straw, or cassies, on their backs to their land' (Wallace 1883, 42: comment added to the 1700 edition). In the fields, it was laid in heaps to wait till time for cultivation arrived (Brand 1701, 19). Composts were also made, for it was noted in 1760 that bere was manured with a compost of earth, seaweed, horse-dung, etc., and that the land was never rested (Pococke 1887, 149). The compost middens were not elongated, pit-like heaps, as they were in Caithness following the innovating Meadowbank system, but cone-shaped, with alternating layers of seaweed and dung mixed with earth, according to an observer in 1774 (Low 1879, 19: Flotta).

The diary of a Sanday farmer, Patrick Fea, records for 23 December 1767: 'My men in the Ware — begun to form beds for the planting of Potatoes' (Fea Diary). Another entry on 25 February 1767 shows that several horses were used for tranport. This must be one of the earliest references in Orkney to ware as a manure for potatoes, which were then only just coming in as a crop. Furthermore, they appear to have been

cultivated in lazy beds, in common with the widespread practice in the
early days of the potato in Scotland.

As elsewhere, detail becomes much fuller from the 1790s. In Cross,
Burness and North Ronaldsay, many more horses and servants were
kept than necessary, in order to recover seaweed for manure when it
came ashore. In fact, sandy soil was not cultivated unless seaware was
available, and sometimes 80 horseloads of seaweed were carried half a
mile to a piece of sandy ground that produced only a boll of bere in
return. Grain grown on fresh seaweed manure weighed less to the boll
than that raised on compost, though a greater quantity was produced
per acre (*OSA* VII (1793), 452, 454). The question of man and animal
power is, of course, one of the important factors that have led to the
disuse of seaweed in more recent times, since horses have ceased to be
readily available for giving access to places too awkward for tractors,
and there are fewer people on the land. At this date, as in Berwickshire
and elsewhere, the seaweed was carried in 'two wooden creels, which
are square and ribbed, and are placed on each side of the horse, the
bottom of which opens, so as to let the ware fall upon the ground it is
intended to manure' (*Ib.*, 471). Straw baskets, however, were used for
carriage on the human back. The island of Westray had forty-five two-
ox carts, and Papa Westray five, for carrying manure (*OSA* XVI
(1795), 253).

In Sandwick and Stromness, seaware was applied in the winter, and
also in spring when the compost dunghills were spread and more fresh
seaweed went on (*OSA* XVI (1795), 420). In Westray the situation was
somewhat similar, seaware being put on after oats, and during winter.
The wared land was ploughed once in spring — which was called
'fallow' — and then bere land got another ploughing after this 'fallow',
before the seed was sown. If ware came ashore fresh it was spread
immediately, but the preference was to ferment it in heaps (*OSA* XVI
(1795), 253). One school of thought considered that seaweed spoiled
grain when used alone, and that it was better composted (Barry 1805,
27). In Shapinsay, it was said that seaweed was applied *after* ploughing,
and the land then sown immediately (*OSA* XVII (1796), 229). In
Kirkwall and St. Ola, fresh or rotten ware was used alone or composted
with turf, and there was no summer fallow to get rid of weeds (*OSA*
VII (1793), 542). Sandy soil, as on the island of Sanday, responded well
to seaware manuring (Forsyth V (1808), 44).

In the nineteenth century new crops and new thinking brought some
variations in practice, but without affecting the intensity of use. In St.

Andrews parish, seaweed, dung and composts of these with earth were the manures (*NSA* XV (1845), 184), but in Lady, seaweed alone was preferred to composts. Where formerly it was carried in creels on horseback, now carts were used (*Ib.*, 145). In Cross and Burness, several oxen were kept for carting seaweed (*Ib.*, 98), and it was still usual for an excess number of horses and oxen to be kept on farms, not in proportion to the needs of farm-work, but to cope with the intensive work of collecting the ware when it came ashore during the 'ware-break', usually in April (Omond, 1911, 6).

In light, sandy soil it was being put on to turnips (*Ib.*, 146) and was much recommended for cabbages, producing plants up to 14 lbs. in weight (*Ib.*, 98). The presence of ware even affected the cropping routine, for it permitted a six-course rotation instead of the more usual rotation of three or four (Farrall 1874, 81).

The improving ideas of the nineteenth century meant that writers sometimes looked with an eye of criticism or censure on earlier practices, amongst others the use of sea ware. Shirreff found that the Orcadians did not make their compost dunghills properly, in spite of their centuries of practice. Their mistake was to put into them the surface turf from their grazing ground (which ruined the pasture), instead of putting in 'gramineous peat' from the mosses. At the same time, however, Shirreff was not quite happy about the incorporation of quick lime in composts, though this seems to have been part of Lord Meadowbank's system. It should presumably have helped to counteract the lack of lime in seaweed (Shirreff 1814, 114-116).

Even though 'sea-weed, to all lands having access to the shore, was the very back bone of the old husbandry' (*Report* 1884, 279), the new husbandry did not disdain it, and indeed there are signs of tighter control of the ware beaches in certain areas, by the landowners to whom the ware belonged. In North Ronaldsay, for instance, laws were drawn up regarding the fair division of seaware for manure in the nineteenth century, by the estate factor. A part of the beach was allocated to each of the six districts or 'toons' in the island, and this part had then to be divided by the crofters themselves on the basis of their rent, acreage, and quality of land, according to rules laid down by the factor. The method of division was simple. A group comprising the half of the members of a 'toon' made a division by sticking tangles upright in the drift, and the other half could then choose whichever side they liked. The dividing and choosing roles were reversed the following year. The same plan was also adopted by the quarters, and by the single shares. This was men's work, and was known as 'the pairting o' the ware' (Scott 1968, 118).

Different methods were used elsewhere. At Aikerness in Evie, three pairs of horses and two pairs of oxen were kept largely for the work on the ware-shore. Each cottar also kept a horse, and a man from each house had to help in the ware. This, along with the threshing of grain, was the main winter job. The ware was transported from the shore in baskets, called *cubbies* or *kaesies*, on the human back, or in hand-barrows, and at Stenso in Evie all the ware was put in four large heaps or *kests*. Those who were carrying the seaweed emptied their burden on to each of the four heaps in succession. At the end, the heaps were balloted for (Omond 1911, 6).

At the Bay of Ireland in Stenness, the landlord 'cut the shores' for kelp, and the tenants got for manure only what the wind blew ashore. In the township of Ireland, according to a description relating to the first half of the eighteenth century, the ware had to be divided between two groups, known as the Bús or bigger farms and the Boons (probably crofts). The Bús were three in number and had priority amongst themselves in a particular order. After them came the six Boons. 'In the division of the ware the Bús and the Boons were said to have so many "shifts". The measuring, which latterly was done by John Smith, of the Hall (one of the Bús), began at the north edge of the burn of Coldomo . . . and proceeded northwards in the following order and measurements: (1) Aglath, 24 fathoms; (2) the six Boons, 24 fathoms among them, to be subdivided by them according to the extent of their respective holdings; (3) the Hall, 24 fathoms; (4) the six Boons, 24 fathoms, to be subdivided as in No. 2; (5) Cumminess, 24 fathoms; (6) the six Boons, 24 fathoms, as before. If more ware was needed, the measurements were repeated in the same order, until the Hall was reached.' Since a number of places claimed all the ware on certain parts below their houses, these parts were omitted from the measurement. Another complication was that the ware sometimes came ashore at one point in a lump, and in this case the measuring could convey a length of clean shore to one or more. This system, no doubt a reflection of the runrig division of the arable, seems to have survived at least till the sale of the township in lots in 1857 (Leask I (1907), 33-34).

Another example relating to Skaill Bay, in the parish of Sandwick, survived till the late nineteenth century. Certain lands in the townships of Northdyke and Scarwell had customary rights to seaweed in proportion to the value of their properties, which were reckoned in *pennylands* (units of land value for taxation purposes). A man from one of these townships *haversed* or divided in two the ware on the beach, and a man from the other got the 'draw', or selection. The next stage was the *thirding* of each half, for each township had three divisions. Each third was eventually subdivided according to the number of *pennylands* claimed by each farmer, and the ware was then piled up in 'ware-middens' above the beach. Into this communal division intruded the question of private right, for Mr Watt of Breckness claimed the seaweed to the South of the burn below the mill of Skaill as his own, as well as that on a certain point north of the burn. This was locally named 'Skaill's ground' (Smith V (1912), 4-5).

An Orkney name recorded for 'a round place above high-water mark, a hollow where each man's seaweed is collected' is *kossel*, a heap of ware is a *kyest*, and a pile of stones used as a boundary mark on the beach, in reference to seaweed division, is a *trip* (Marwick 1929, s.v.). A rake with which ware was dragged ashore, or spread on the land, was a *klooro* (*Ib.*, s.v.).

In the late nineteenth-early twentieth century, a farmer in the island of Stronsay, called Tait, kept a diary year by year. From this it is possible to make a fairly detailed reconstruction of the seasonal involvement with ware. The following table shows the number of days worked per month at the ware, whether for manure or for kelp-burning. Some allowance must be made for irregularity in the keeping of the Diaries.

Days Worked per Month on Ware

Month	1896	1900	1905	1907	1908	1909	1910	1911	1912	1914	1916	1918
J	1	6	—	1	2	13	10	12	8	4	14	—
F	—	5	3	4	4	5	—	4	3	5	4	—
M	—	4	15	7	5	—	2	9	1	4	1	1
A	—	—	1	1	2	2	1	—	—	—	9	—
M	—	—	—	—	—	—	—	1	—	—	—	—
J	—	1	—	—	—	—	—	—	—	—	2	1
J	—	—	—	—	—	—	—	—	—	—	—	—
A	—	3	—	—	1	5	3	1	6	6	1	—
S	—	—	—	—	—	—	—	—	1	—	1	1
O	—	—	—	—	—	—	5	1	—	—	—	—
N	—	—	1	—	6	1	12	10	—	4	6	8
D	7	—	6	—	3	1	12	3	3	3	1	7

The table shows clearly that the ware comes ashore chiefly in

November, December, January, February and March, and with an occasional late storm in April. By far the greater proportion of time was taken on carting ware. The spreading which followed was quickly done.

A distinction is usually made between the littoral ware and the sublittoral tang, the former being spread immediately for the most part, the latter going into middens. Ware is further divided into fresh and rotten ware, the latter presumably kept in heaps, to be applied chiefly in March before 'corn', which in Orkney is an abbreviation for 'bere-corn', i.e. bere or barley.

In April 'kelp ware' was gathered and was burned in the course of May and June. The finished product was carted to the store at the pier in August for shipment. After that the round of carting tang and ware began again, but the practice here shows that the demands on seaweed for kelp and for manure did not conflict. This was past the heyday of kelp-burning, however, and the kelp was burned as a little extra for the farm income.

The quantities involved may be realised from the fact that up to nine carts could be at work at once, and up to twenty loads a day are specified. Not every year was equally good — for example on 1 January 1916 Tait commented that a wet December had produced little ware, only about sixty loads. The incidence of wind and storms, after which large quantities of ware became available, can be seen from the months when a large number of days were absorbed by the work.

The pattern of use in Shetland is less intense than in Orkney for the reason that seaweed comes ashore there in lesser quantities. There, it was spread fresh if its arrival coincided with the spring work of cultivation and sowing. At other times, in autumn and winter, it could only be used in the best way by being composted with earth or dung (Shirreff 1814, 55). This undoubtedly did happen, but the impression gained from a perusal of the sources is that seaweed was a much less frequent element of compost dunghills than in Orkney.

Nevertheless, ware was of great value, and its absence affected the value of land away from the coast (Brand 1701, 66), for the numerous Shetland ponies or 'shelties', whose only work was said to be to carry seaweed for manure (Anon. 1750, 9), do not seem to have carried it very far. The beaches were divided out in the usual way, and squabbling over them is recorded from at least 1602, when the three sisters in Stobreck were fined for the 'wrangous gripster (seizure) of William Smithis wair' (Donaldson 1954, 16). Regulations about not taking bait (for fishing) or cutting tang in another man's ebb were noted in the old Country Acts about 1725 (Gifford 1879, 78). In the 1880s, evidence given to the Crofters Commission by Major T. M. Cameron of Garth and Annsbrae said that the proprietor reserved to himself all peat-mosses, seaweed and shell sand on his property, with power to regulate and divide these as necessary. The drift and seaweed for manure was to be divided amongst the tenants according to the quantity of land held by each. All other seaweed was reserved by the proprietor (*Report* 1884, Appx. A, II, 231). However, this system was breaking down by the 1930s, when the Board of Trade advertised that farmers and crofters could take seaweed from any part of the foreshore in Unst without restriction, whereas under the old udal system of land tenure each farm and croft had its own stretch (Sandison 1968, 13).

In the 1790s the three primary types of manure in use for bere were a compost of byre and stable manure and peat mould, sometimes with seaweed added; byre manure allowed to accumulate in the byre; and the seaweed itself, usually heaped up in March and April and left to rot before being applied (Low 1879, 161-2). The compost dunghills, made on the outfields in winter, were said to be small (*OSA* VII (1793), 586: Sandsting and Aithsting). In Delting, tang was a general and successful manure (*OSA* I (1791), 390), and in Unst tang and seaware were used wherever they could be got (*OSA* V (1793), 192).

An early nineteenth-century comment that the composting of byre dung and earth with seaweed was more common than the use of seaweed alone (Forsyth V (1808), 126-7) is reinforced by parish accounts from the middle of the century. The pattern given for Sandsting and Aithsting fifty years before still prevailed. At seedtime, the compost was dug down and well mixed with the spade, being carried from the heaps in *cashies* or baskets on the human back. It was spread out by hand. All the ground dug in one day was sown, manured, and harrowed in the evening (*NSA* XV (1845), 118). By this date, in fact, there may have been some falling off in the use of seaware, for the cultivation of bere as a crop was dying out. This may also be indicated by the fact that, at least in part, seaware had come to be regarded as the manure for the cottars (*NSA* XV (1845), 158). There was, therefore, not so much a sinking of seaweed manuring in the social scale, as a fossilisation of the practice at a particular social level. This was only partially true, however, for seaweed remained in wide use for long afterwards, for example as a top-dressing for grass and arable. Even so, however, it was not spread fresh, but was either

Fig. 17. Redware spread as manure on a *rig* at the Wirlie, Papa Stour, Shetland. AF 1967.

Fig. 18. A compost dunghill of seaweed and byre-manure, known as a *muck-roog*, at the Wirlie, Papa Stour, Shetland. AF 1967.

allowed to rot in heaps for three months, or was composted with cow dung, earth, and fish-offal (Skirving 1874, 201-2).

In April 1967, during a field research trip to the island of Papa Stour, a field was seen, cultivated by the spade, with a layer of red-ware from the shore spread over it (Fig. 17). Bere was to be sown there in May. There was also a *muck-roog* (dunghill) in the middle of one field at the croft of The Wirlie, built up in a squarish shape, of alternate layers of seaweed and byre manure (Fig. 18). Not every croft used seaweed, but formerly it was a March job to collect it and pile it up in *roogs* or heaps below the banks. After carts came into use, the seaweed was piled above the banks since the carts could not go down. The women carried the ware in *kishies* or baskets on their backs, and the men forked it up into the *roogs*. This work was a common task, and when it was done, there came the *pairtin' o' the waar*, one pile being built for every house. The piles were left for a day or two, and then the seaweed was carried to the cultivation *rigs* or small fields, in the *kishies*. Here, they were built up into dunghills with alternating layers of byre-manure, and the *muck roogs* were finished off with a layer of broken up turf. This system had been in common use till very recently, but the Wirlie *muck roog* was almost the last of the line. There was no indication, in discussions of the seasonal round of work, that seaweed was gathered at times other than March.

The Western Highlands and Islands

It is in this region, but especially in the Hebrides, that seaweed remains in most active use in Scotland. Since the Hebrides have their own kind of character, and since the county boundary that splits Lewis and Harris is rather artificial, they will be considered as a unit in this survey.

As far as the mainland is concerned, little information has come to hand for Sutherland prior to the 1790s. Tang and 'kelp ware' were the commonest types, with another 'resembling kelp ware, of an unctuous appearance, so very rich, that it must be cut into small pieces, and spread thin, otherwise the crop would be too luxuriant'. This was called *femman nam partan*, 'crab-ware', in Gaelic (*OSA* III (1792), 531: Tongue). In Durness, red-ware was used (*OSA* III (1792), 577), and in Edderachyllis the great profusion of seaware made the best manure, especially when cut early in spring and mixed with earth (*OSA* VI

(1793), 289). In Loth, seaware answered best for bere (*OSA* VI (1793), 313-314).

In Assynt, seaweed was used where available (*OSA* XVI (1795), 186), and this may partly explain why in 'the 1770s the distinction between coastal and inland farms was a fundamental fact in the agriculture of Assynt' (Adam 1960, xliv). The rentals of the coastal farms were consistently higher. Ardvare farm was one referred to where the infields were rocky and full of baulks, but had the advantage of seaware (*Ib.*, 7). Bellachlattack had dry sandy soil, easily manured with seaware (*Ib.*, 11), and Oldernay, perhaps the best farm on the Assynt estate, had some remarkably fertile fields, 'which may be owing to their vicinity to the Sea Ware, that excellent Manure being easily got in great plenty from that large sandy Creek of the Sea called the Ebb adjoining these grounds' (*Ib.*, 42).

Little is said of the work involved in gathering and transporting seaweed, but no doubt the women who carried the creels felt no little relief when a track was made to the creek at Farr about 1880, so that the crofters could cart their seaweed (*Report* 1884, Appx. A, LXIV, 294).

In Mainland Ross, much seaware was used in Applecross (*OSA* III (1792), 374). In Kintail and Glenshiel the tenants had the privilege of taking what they needed for their barley and potatoes. Kelp was made with the rest (*OSA* VI (1793), 252; *OSA* VII (1793), 127). The soil at Tarbat had been made open by the frequent use of seaweed, mainly for bere, but also for pease, oats, and rye, and attempts were made to give it more firmness with a mixture of seaweed dug in with black earth and gravel (*OSA* VI (1793), 420). In Lochbroom seaweed was the commonest manure, and there were also some compost dunghills (*OSA* X (1794), 462).

By the 1840s some changes had begun to take place, for in Glenshiel dung rather than seaweed was being used with the bere crop (*NSA* XIV (1845), 205), and in Applecross the manure was compound dunghills, shell-sand, seaware, and a little lime (*Ib.*, 102).

Few data have been noted for the West Mainland of Inverness, though seaweed was sometimes got with no little labour. Men from Poolewe would go in the rough weather of March and April to cut tangle on the coast of the Rudha Reidh promontory, ten miles out to sea, to get manure for their potatoes. On shore they carried it two miles on their backs up a steep hill to the cultivated spots on the moor (Mackenzie 1949, 154-155).

As far as the Hebrides are concerned, some early and interesting information is available. In 1549, Lewis was described as being covered with peat moss right down to the seacoast. In the place where peats were dried one year — i.e. on a raised bank of peat — the bere was sown in the following year, well manured with seaware (Munro 1961, 87). In Little Bernera, too, where seaware abounded, a great deal of bere was annually grown by spade cultivation alone (*Ib.*, 81). It is likely that these comments point to an early stage in the development of lazybed cultivation in peaty soils. Evidence adduced from other areas in relation to composts shows that seaware makes a good combination with peat-moss, which is the typical lazybed base.

It is also characteristic that seaware must be applied every year, since its good effects do not carry over. It is no light task to continually keep a productive heart in ground covered by many feet of peat. A visitor to Callernish in Lewis will readily appreciate a comment of a hundred years ago, that: 'Except peat, the soil contains nothing but what has been put into it by hard labour, viz. — seaware gathered from the shore, rotten straw taken from the roofs of cottages, the proceeds of byre and stable, etc.; but at the end of all the centuries since Callernish was made, and during which it has been fed and nourished by the people, the land is very little better than the miles and miles of black peat-bog that extend around it on all sides' (Carruthers 1875-80, 185).

Yet considerable numbers of people were maintained by good use of the available resources, amongst them the indispensable seaweed, equally useful for peat and for sandy or light gravelly soils. It was estimated in the early 1800s, that seaweed constituted a half of all the manure in the Hebrides, and up to nine-tenths of that in the remoter islands. Normally applied to barley, spread three to five inches deep, it produced a good yield even on ground successively cropped for many years without a rest. A seed-yield ratio of 1:16 or 17 was noted (Macdonald 1811, 403-406), well above contemporary Mainland figures, but this is a higher figure than the average.

Though in general use, seaware was nevertheless 'very grossly mismanaged', in the opinion of an economic historian. He disapproved of leaving the seaweed spread without being ploughed in, and thought it better if it was heaped, and if possible mixed with sea-sleech, for one to four months (Walker I (1812), 154-6). This implies that heaping, and composting, was not much of a Hebridean characteristic, and though compost dunghills were made in the islands — for example, in Barra (*OSA* XIII (1794), 330) — they were nothing like as general as on the Highland mainland (cf. Robertson 1808, 239) and in the Northern Isles. Whereas in other parts of Scotland, all other work tended to stop in order to rescue a new landing of seaweed, here it was left to lie if other work was pressing. The smell of the seaweed heating and putrifying on the shore was 'strong and offensive to a degree'. If they could, the Hebrideans removed and spread the seaweed at once, though 'the people are aware that much of the substance of the seaweed is thus lost to them. But they cannot do better' (*Report* 1884, Appx. A, XCIX, 467).

Several types and qualities of seaweed were distinguished. Macdonald mentioned *feamuin dhubh* or black seaware, exposed on the littoral for eight hours out of every twelve; *buiag*, or yellow seaware, exposed for only four out of each twelve hours, and *braggaire*, or crackling seaware, a sub-littoral type, rarely cut by hand like the two first-mentioned varieties, but cast up by storms. *Braggaire* (*am bragaire*) was the best manure if got fresh, but as a rule it was spoiled by the time it reached the shore. Being thought unfit for kelp, it was left as manure for the tenants' lands. *Buiag* (*buidheag*) was the strongest, and the preferable manure, but for the most part it, and the *feamuin dhubh* (*feamainn dubh*) were kept for kelp. In terms of relative strength, a ridge of potatoes requiring ten cartloads of *buigheag* would need twelve of *feamainn dubh* and fourteen or fifteen of *braggaire* (Macdonald 1811, 238-239). A fourth type mentioned was *glurach*, probably *gleadhrach*, a 'kind of knotted seaweed, used for cuttings' (Dwelly 1949, s.v.). These four names cover the species *Fucus vesiculosus*, *F. nodosus*, *F. serratus*, and *F. digitatus* (Macdonald 1811, 403).

Drifted seaweed used for manure was called *sgùilleach*, i.e. rubbish (Macdonald XXXVII (1934), 23-24). This term as used at present on the West side of Lewis refers to a mixture of all kinds of seaweed. The general Gaelic name for seaweed is *feamainn*. The red or tangle seaweed, often called *bruchd*, was cast up and left to ferment. The cutting seaweed was *an fheamainn*.

In Uist the red seaweed was distinguished as *feamainn dearg* or *bàrr dearg*, and the black seaweed, which was cut, was *feamainn dubh*. Red seaweed cast ashore in May, June and July (of which kelp was made) was *am bragaire*. The cutting seaweed, *an fheamainn ghearraidh*, was divided into various types: *feamainn dubh*, which did not float, *fheamainn bhuidhe* or *bhuidheagach* which floated, *gleadhrach*, which floated, and *feamainn chìrean* or *chìreag*, the latter used as a laxative for cattle.

Ripe seaweed cast ashore was *feamainn-chura*, and decomposed seaweed used to manure the ground after it had rotted was *f.-phuil*.

The verb *a'feamnaidh* was applied to manuring with seaweed, or to carrying the seaweed from the shore to the land (Dwelly 1949, s.v. *feamainn*; McDonald 1958, 301 (list of seaweed terms)). This wide and varied nomenclature, of which the examples given here constitute a selection, shows clearly enough in itself the essential part that seaweed played in the economy of the area.

Since the nature of the soil, whether peaty or sandy, made seaweed an absolute necessity, and since little attempt seems to have been made to store it by composting for spring cultivation, the annual throwing up by the sea of seaweed in quantities was a matter of great importance. In 1703 a curious account was published of a ritual which aimed at ensuring a plentiful supply. The inhabitants of Lewis sacrificed to 'a Sea God *Shony*, at Hallowtide, in the manner following. The Inhabitants round the Island came to the Church of *St Mulvay*, having each Man his Provision along with him; every Family furnish'd a Peck of Malt, and this was brew'd into Ale; one of their number was pickt out to wade into the Sea up to the middle, and carrying a Cup of Ale in his Hand, standing still in that posture, cry'd out with a loud voice, saying, SHONY *I give you this Cup of Ale, hoping that you'll be so kind as to send us plenty of Sea-Ware for inriching our Ground the ensuing year*; and threw the Cup of Ale into the Sea. This was perform'd in the Night-Time; at his return to Land they all went to the Church, where there was a Candle burning upon the Altar; and then standing silent for a little time, one of them gave a Signal, at which the Candle was put out, and immediately all of them went to the Fields, where they fell a drinking their Ale, and spent the remainder of the Night in Dancing and Singing, etc.' (Martin (1703) 1884, 28).

Whatever may be thought of the mythological content, there can be no doubt that the anxiety for seaweed was real enough, and in fact the custom is known from later sources. It was said that on Maundy Thursday the coast dwellers made offerings of mead, ale, or gruel to the god of the sea. As the morning of the Thursday dawned a man walked into the sea as Martin described, made the libation and chanted:

A Dhe na mara,	O God of the sea,
Cuir todhar's an tarruinn	Put weed in the drawing ware
Chon tachair an talaimh	To enrich the ground
Chon bailcidh dhuinn biaidh	To shower on us food.

Those on shore also took up the chant, 'the darkness of night and the rolling of the waves making the scene weird and impressive'. The custom was within the oral memory of a middle-aged man in the island of Iona in 1860, his father having taken part in the ceremony when young (Carmichael I (1928), 162-3).

Shortage of seaweed due to a calm period was regarded as a serious matter, and a simple prayer for seaweed was sung then:

Toradh mara gu tìr,	Produce of sea to land,
Toradh tìre gu muir:	Produce of land to sea:
Neach nach deàn'na ìr,	He who doeth not in time,
Crìon gum bi a chuid.	Scant shall be his share.
Feamainn 'ga cur gu tìr,	Seaweed being cast on shore,
Builich, a Thì na buil;	Bestow, Thou Being of bestowal:
Toradh ga chur an nì,	Produce being brought to wealth,
A Chrìosda, thoir mo chuid.	O Christ, grant me my share!

When wind and sea renewed the supply, a prayer was sung:

Thàine 's gun tàine feamainn,	Come and come is seaweed,
Thàine 's gun tàine brùchd,	Come and come is red seaware,
Thàine buidheag 's thàine liaghag,	Come is yellow weed, come is tangle,
Thàine biadh mu'n iadh an stùc.	Come is food which the ware enwraps.
Thàinig Micheal mìl na conail,	Come is warrior Michael of fruitage,
Thàinig Brighde bhìth na ciùin,	Come is womanly Brigit of gentleness,
Thàinig a' Mhàthair mhìn Mhoire,	Come is the mild Mother Mary,
'S thàinig Connan àigh an iùil.	And come is glorious Connan of guidance.

(Carmichael IV (1941), 32-35).

As regards the division of the seaweed on the shore, it is likely that the great emphasis on kelp-burning in the late eighteenth–early nineteenth centuries has obscured and modified the earlier situation. The Crofters Commission Report in 1884 throws light on this through its recommendations, one of which states that the township should possess a preferential right to cutting and gathering seaware without payment on and for the township lands (except for kelp, which should remain in the hands of the owner of the land). If seaweed was scarce in any area, the tenants should have access to seaweed on the shores adjacent to the township belonging to the proprietor and occupied by him or his tenant (*Report* 1884, 19-23). Thus the proprietor's rights were modified, as far as the seaweed on the beach was concerned.

Offshore, however, it was said that anyone could cut seaweed from a boat without hindrance, and in Skye it is on record that a kind of tangle, *leathagan*, rarely used for kelp, was cut during spring tides and carried to land in boats for spreading fresh on barley and potatoes (*OSA* XVI (1795), 153: Portree).

The communal situation indicated by the rituals recorded by Martin and Carmichael goes with a period when the land was worked on the *runrig* system, a kind of joint farming. When this came to an end in the course of the late eighteenth but more usually in the nineteenth century, the clustered villages were replaced by dispersed groups of small farms or crofts, each standing on its own piece of land, which usually ran in a strip from the shore below to the hill dyke behind. With this reorganisation, the seaweed rights normally went to the crofter whose land touched the shore, but if it happened that a croft had the whole of a beach, this would have to be divided with neighbours.

On the East Coast of Harris, each township group had a stretch of shore allocated by the proprietor or tacksman. Here much of the seaweed had to be cut, at low water, and was carried by all the tenants together above the flood mark, on their backs. It was laid in heaps, whose numbers corresponded to those of the tenants on the farms, and then they cast lots for them. Afterwards the tenants carried the heaps they had got to their own plots of ground, which they had also got by lot. It was said that it took about 200 large creelfuls of seaweed to produce a boll of barley or twelve to fourteen barrels of potatoes (*OSA* X (1794), 352-3: Harris).

Both before and after the days of joint runrig farming, of the kind indicated here, the work of seaweed sharing was closely controlled. In the Outer Hebrides, for example, the constable or officer of the township would not allow a crofter to cart seaweed from the shore until his neighbours had had a reasonable allowance of time to get there. Nor would he allow a crofter to cut where and when he liked. He also saw to it that in transporting seaweed from the shore, which is very heavy work, no one should work his horse too heavily or for too long (*Report*, 1884, Appx. A, XLVIII, 216, XCIX, 454).

Rules for division were not necessarily firmly adhered to when seaweed was plentiful, but when it was scarce, the shore was divided — as in Orkney — into *peighinnean*, 'pennies', in proportion to the number of ridges or *rigs* of land held by the crofter. Another part of the organisation was the man called *am peursair*, the 'perchman'. He was

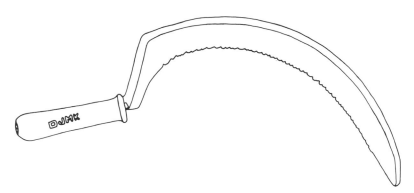

Fig. 19. A seaweed sickle from the Hebrides. In NMAS (No. PB 2).

employed by the township to keep an eye on the shore, and when seaweed arrived, he hoisted a bundle of seaweed on a pole as a sign to the rest, who would then come with horse, carts, and creels to rescue it, often overloading themselves and their animals in the process. The perchman got his pay in a proportion of seaweed, and in land (*Report*, 1884, Appx. A, XCIX, 467).

The cutting of seaweed is usually done by means of a sickle with a smooth blade, or sometimes with tough teeth knocked out in it. A seaweed sickle was called *corran gearraidh* (Fig. 19).

Transport of the seaweed was done in a variety of ways. It could be in a boat to the shore, if sub-littoral weed had been cut, or it could be made into rafts and towed ashore, letting the rising tide do the work. This is a method also used in Ireland (O'Neill VIII (1970, 17 ff; Evans 1957, 221-4). A heap of cut seaweed lying on the shore, well bound with ropes, ready to float on the tide so that it could be towed to the owners' croft, was known as a *maois-feamann* (Macdonald XXXVII (1934), 23-24), *maois* or *ball* (Dwelly 1949, s.v. *maois* and *fasda*). At one time the ropes used to tie such a bundle were made of heather (McDonald 1958, 174). The towing rope itself was the *fasda* (Dwelly 1949, s.v.). The second stage in transport was getting it from the shore to the land, and here the methods varied according to the terrain and social status. The natives of Berneray, Barra, for example, carried seaware in ropes on their backs over high rocks (Martin (1703) 1884, 94), but creels on the human back or on horseback were more usual. Carts were used where conditions allowed. Back creels seem to have been the ordinary wicker creels of the area, piled up high. In this present century sacks have sometimes been used, for 'in Boreray, we have witnessed a small procession of women ascending from a geo (creek) and laden with sea-ware in sacks slung across their shoulders' (Beveridge 1911, 325-326). The popular idea of women being the main beasts of burden for carrying the seaweed from shore to cultivation beds in creels on their backs is exaggerated, for certainly men did it as well, and a great many horses were used at one time. However, as sheep farming was developed by the proprietors, the tenants were deprived more and more of hill pasture, and with it the possibility of maintaining a number of ponies for seaweed work. As a result the women were increasingly left to do this work from the late eighteenth century onwards (*Report*, 1884, Appx. A, V, 11: Skye), though horses were not given up by any means, and it could still be said in the mid-nineteenth century in Lewis that 'their principal work is in carrying peats and sea-ware in creels, one hung on each side from the crook-saddle' (*NSA* XIV (1845), 122: Stornoway, Lewis). The creels used on horses appear to have been D-shaped with a flat side that lay against the horse. A pad or mat of plaited bent-grass or later of coir-yarn went across the pony's back as a protection. These creels were made of wood and wickerwork (see Fig. 11 in Fenton 1973, 139), and had a 'somewhat complicated attachment' by which the bottom could be released to let the load out (Beveridge 1911, 326). Not all creels could be emptied in this way, and for both loading and unloading, an equal balance had to be maintained at each side. For this reason, the work of carrying seaweed in creels on the backs of horses required at least two people if it was to be done efficiently. Not only were the creels filled, but the seaweed was also to some extent piled over the horse's back and roped down if necessary (see Shaw 1955, Plate 3b). In Sutherland, the seaweed was carried in creels on horseback, or in '*crubans* (a triangular machine made of wood for that purpose)' (Henderson 1812, 95-6).

Prior to the second half of the eighteenth century, the seaweed was chiefly used for manuring the barley crops, on the best land, which, especially when cultivated in the form of lazybeds, sometimes received little rest. In this, such beds were little different from the ordinary kitchen garden, which goes on producing year after year if manured well enough. However, the overwhelming dependence that gradually came to be placed on the potato crop, and the need to fertilise this well, meant that barley or rather bere was more and more neglected in certain areas, to the point sometimes of extinction (*OSA* XVI (1795), 535-6; Sleat, Skye). This was not true everywhere, for a large sandy tract at the north end of South Uist, for example, was brought under cultivation in the nineteenth century and was producing about 150 acres of bere on the abundant seaweed manure available there (*NSA* XIV (1845), 192). It was said in Barra that the best potatoes came from the seaweed first laid on the ground in November, though it was laid down at all periods between then and the end of May (*Ib.*, 212). Whether the seaweed was cut, or blown ashore, it was still used for potatoes (*Ib.*, 153: Small Isles).

The labour involved in gathering and transporting seaweed scarcely needs to be emphasised. To carry the 160 creels thought necessary for an acre was no easy task (Moisley 1962, 74). It is mainly because of this that its use has declined so fast in this present century. As recently as 1955, a survey showed that in North-West Scotland, only 34 out of 168 townships with coastal access were using it. Scarcity of horses to provide transport in creels or in carts, allied with the frequently rocky nature of the shores, a dwindling population with fewer people able or willing to undertake the heavy work of carrying on the back, and the fact that the preferred seaweed variety, *Fucus*, had to be cut in several places, have all been factors contributing to its decline. In Skye, where only 50% of the townships that could have used it did so, the problems were similar. In the Outer Isles, especially in the southern parts, the tangle, *Laminaria*, was the main seaweed, cast ashore in plenty by prevailing westerly winds, and applied to the shell-sand *machair*, where it remedied deficiencies in potash and organic matter. The same was true of Tiree in Argyll. The standards of husbandry have undoubtedly declined where seaweed is scarce or not used (Darling 1955, 214).

The abandonment of seaweed is also in part due to the availability of artificial fertilisers, which are bought in spite of heavy freight charges. This is made clear, for example, from a study of the Bernera district of Lewis in 1962, when it appeared that out of 99 crofts, all used artificial fertiliser and dung, 58 used lime, 48 used seaweed, 3 used shell sand, and 10 used nothing at all. The part played by Government legislation in this picture should not be forgotten, for a certain amount of artificial fertiliser has to be applied before the ploughing subsidy can be claimed (Moisley 1962, 74-75).

West-Central and South-West Scotland

The county of Argyll includes a number of islands, some of which, like Jura and Colonsay, depended entirely on seaweed. From it, only one crop could be got, and this, it was suggested, 'answers the contracted views of the farmer, who keeps the best patches of his ground constantly in tillage, and labours like one who is not certain of his possession beyond the present year' (*OSA* XII (1794), 321). In Tiree, over two-thirds of the manure was seaweed (*OSA* X (1794), 396).

As in other districts, agricultural writers approved of it as a manure, but disapproved of its treatment. The best effects were achieved if it was laid on in April or May, rather than in winter, which must have been the common practice. Careful farmers in the late eighteenth century spread what came ashore in summer on ley-ground, or heaped it. It was thought, however, that composting would be better (Smith 1798, 201-2). Curiously enough, it was in areas where seaweed was comparatively scarce and of inferior quality that composting or mixing with dung was practised (*OSA* III (1792), 174: Lochgoilhead and Kilvorich).

In the parish of Inverchaolain there appears to have been a reversal of the usual pattern, for here seaweed was applied to oats, and dung to the bere crop (*OSA* V (1793), 466). In other parishes, such as Strachur, and Kilmartin, it was applied as usual to bere and potatoes (*OSA* III (1792), 558; *OSA* VIII (1793), 93).

In Kilfinichen and Kilvickeon, the seaweeds were specified as button wrack, lady wrack, black ware, and tangle. All were used for manure, and for mossy ground proved to be the only useful type of manure. Button and lady wrack were burned for kelp if the price of kelp was high, but if not, they also served as manure (*OSA* XIV (1795), 181-2). There was obviously a close eye kept on the balance between the need for manure and the manufacture of kelp, for the Duke of Argyll's factor noted in a report on kelp in Mull that the main manure was black wrack and tangle, interspersed with yellow or kelp ware. It was cut every spring. There was some encroachment on the kelp ware for manure if the price of kelp was low and oatmeal likely to be dear, and conversely the seaweeds of less value for kelp were burned by the cottars and others if the price of kelp was high. The factor wrote in 1796 that 'this necessary connection . . . betwixt the management of the shores and the cultivation of the soil . . . cannot be broken through without evident injury to the tenants in the first instance, and ultimately to my Lord Duke'. He recommended that the tenants of Mull and Morvern should be left to work the shores themselves, either for kelp or manure, according to the market (Cregeen 1964, 189-192). A further suggestion was that the island of Calve should be made useful to the settlement of Tobermory, founded as a planned village in 1788, by obliging the possessor to give the whole black wrack and tangle annually for manure to the settlers, at an annual suggested price of 20/- a year (*Ib.*, 172, 174, 177).

In mid-nineteenth century Mull, when the small tenants and crofters were still planting their potatoes in lazybeds, it was found that potatoes grown on seaware were not as dry as those planted or dibbled in lazybeds, and manured with dung (*NSA* VII (1845), 308).

In the Firth of Clyde, the island of Arran in the county of Bute, famous for potatoes 'uncommonly farinaceous, and of fine flavour', made good use of seaweed manure (Headrick 1807, 331-2). At the head of the same Firth, in the county of Dumbarton, seaweed was also used for potatoes, either by itself or in composts. It was laid rather thickly on lazybeds, and the seed cuttings were put immediately above it. The potatoes so grown, however, were 'commonly wet, ill tasted, and not prolific', perhaps, it was suggested, because the seaweed was not properly rotted first (Ure 1794).

In the farming practice of Dumbarton some years later, two types of seaweed were used. The first was 'cut wreck', cut with sickles every second spring off large stones at low tide, when it was in a vigorous state of growth, and highly impregnated with sea salt. This made it a powerful manure. It was spread thinly when got from the beach, and was ploughed down immediately. The second type, 'blown or drift wreck', was more plentiful but less valuable, and got especially in winter (as well as throughout the year). Some spread it at once, and ploughed it down the following spring, but it was best put in heaps and allowed to rot, when it helped to destroy weed, whereas freshly gathered and spread seaweed did not. It was also composted, for the same reason, with stable and byre dung, and fermented well. It was good for barley and turnips, and also for potatoes, though rarely used for them (Whyte and Macfarlan 1811, 194-6).

In the next county of Renfrew, seaweed was cut for barley at the beginning of May. It was thought to be poorer than wind-driven seaweed, though still very productive. The latter was also applied to barley, as well as to oats and potatoes (*OSA* V (1793), 561: Greenock). In Port Glasgow parish, seaweed was not much used by the best farmers, who depended on cows and their produce for the payment of rent rather than on cropping and did not have good access to the shore from their hill farms (*Ib.*, 546).

With its relatively long coastline. Ayrshire had good opportunities to get supplies of this resource, and the privilege of getting it was jealously guarded. In January 1700, William Fullerton raised a 'Decreet Absolvitur & Declarator Anent the priviledge of lifting Wrack and Ware from the Sea Shoar' before the Lords of Session, against the Laird of Adamton, Monktoun and Monktounhill, who claimed the privilege of 'lifting and away Carrying of Wrack and Ware upon the Shoar opposite to the Lands belonging to the said William Fullerton'. The Lords declared in favour of the latter, as having the sole privilege (Macfarlane II (1900), 349-350).

In 1730, the burgh of Prestwick had to forbid the gathering of seaware at any time on the Sabbath day (Fullerton 1834, 89), as in North-East Scotland, so indicating the anxiety of the farmers to rescue this manure.

In the 1790s, the parishes of Ayr (*OSA* I (1791), 92), Ballantrae (*Ib.*, 113), Girvan (*OSA* XII (1794), 336), the Cumbraes (*Ib.*, 393), Stevenston (*OSA* VII (1793), 6), and Dundonald (*Ib.*, 622, 625) are mentioned as using seaweed. At a slightly later period, it was said that much seaweed was used, but in a rather slovenly way, much being allowed to rot on the beach before it was spread. On the Horse Isle particularly it was heaped up and neglected for ages, many thousand cartloads being left to lie rotted and neglected. Only those whose land reached to the shore had a right to it (Aiton 1811, 386).

One of the interesting pieces of organisation on this coast, based on Monkton, was an institution among the farmers called the 'Wreck Brethren Society'. It existed between 1796 and 1887. The Society 'served a good purpose in keeping up the roads and bridges leading to the shore. As officebearers, they had a President and generally four Bailies. Annually they raised funds for their purposes, and regulated the carting of the *wreck*'. They met at different places, a private house, the schoolhouse, or the inn, and certainly mixed pleasure with business, for the accounts for 23 December 1848 include 'to whisky and bakes 4/6' (Hewat 1894, 112-3).

In Ayrshire, seaweed became more and more of an ancillary to dung, however, especially in the potato-growing districts near Girvan, and on the early farms of Ardrossan and West Kilbride. When spread and ploughed down, not only did it have a fertilising affect, but its salt content also helped to save crops on sandy soil in times of drought (*Report* 1878, 71-2).

It remained in use until very recently in Ayrshire, especially for potatoes.

In the extreme South-West, Wigtownshire with its extensive coastline has produced surprisingly few records. In Sorbie, some seaweed was spread fresh, but the best farmers composted it to induce a quick, strong fermentation (*OSA* I (1791), 246). In Stonykirk, south-east winds brought seaweed in plenty to Balgreggan head, in Luce Bay. It was regularly applied as a manure, and would produce one luxuriant crop on wet clay, especially if the summer that followed was dry and warm (*OSA* II (1792), 52).

In general it was regarded here as a good manure when ploughed down in a moist state, but otherwise composting was preferred. It was said that, though a good top-dressing for barley, when applied just after the grain was sown, this technique was not much known to the Galloway farmers. It was also recommended as a top dressing on pasture land (Smith 1810, 217).

In Wigtownshire, the proprietors gave the tenants the exclusive right to seaweed on their own farms, and also allowed any tenant on the estate to cart as much as he liked. This privilege was, for some reason, not granted in Kirkcudbrightshire, where seaweed was often left to lie rotting unused (Smith 1810, 216-217).

Conclusion

This historical circumnavigation of the Scottish coast was intended to assemble some of the very scattered data in the first instance. Much remains to be done, and in the meantime many gaps in the evidence lie unfilled. However, enough has been gathered to show that seaweed is or rather was a resource common to all the coastal parts of Scotland, capable of being integrated into farming on a big scale as well as into small-scale crofting. The reasons for its abandonment at different periods have been outlined in the regional sections; but the fact remains that a detailed study of any primary resource such as this can produce an incisive pointer to the work organisation in the areas of its use. In this case, because of its widespread use, it allows for comparisons between the different areas of Scotland, keeping them all in balance, in a way that is often forgotten or ignored.

4
Paring and Burning

Early evidence for paring and burning as a means of fertilising arable land is almost non-existent in Scotland, though the burning of heath and moors to improve grazing goes back at least to the sixteenth century under the name of *muirburn*. It is amply recorded from that period, usually because its careless use had led, as in Moray, to 'the numberless instances of houses, corns, woods, etc. destroyed' (*Caledonian Mercury*, 26 March 1764). Already in 1773 there was national legislation against its indiscriminate practice, and it was decreed that 'every Person who shall make Muirburn, or set fire to any Heath or Muir, in that part of *Great Britain* called *Scotland*, from the Eleventh Day of *April* to the First Day of *November* in any Year, shall forfeit and pay the Sum of Forty Shillings Sterling' (*AP*, 13 George III, Ch. 54, para. 4). In addition, there was a good deal of local legislation, for example on the estate of Urie in Kincardineshire where an instruction was given at the Baron Court in 1724 that no tenants, cottars, grassmen, their servants, or children, were to burn any mosses or moors in the Barony, and in 1733 proceedings were taken against persons for 'kindling of mureburn, fire raising, and burning the mosses and mures' (Barron 1892, 125, 151).

To judge by the geographical spread of references given in the *Scottish National Dictionary* and the *Dictionary of the Older Scottish Tongue*, muirburn was probably a fairly widespread practice in pre-enclosure days, in the moorland areas of eastern Scotland and in the Southern Uplands. From there, the practice of controlled heather burning followed the sheep as they spread into the Highlands, so that in 1799, for instance, one writer could speak of the improvement by burning of Cruachan in Argyll, for sheep grazing, 'in imitation of the south country practice' (Smith I (1799), 237). It is this spread that is the subject of legislation like the Hill Farming Act of 1946, enforcing adequate numbers of people and sufficient equipment to control heather burning.

The use of fire to clear a top growth of heath and rank grass is thus widespread and well attested from the sixteenth century. Although the purpose now is to improve the grazing, formerly it may just as often have been to clear ground for the turf or *flauchter* spade. The early evidence for the cutting of turf with spades or ploughs, and its subsequent burning, is not so straightforward, however. It is certain that in the late eighteenth century it was not much practised except on the estates of improving landlords, very much as in England. Some writers said it had been anciently in general use, though none adduced positive evidence, and the sources so far noted do not take it back beyond the mid-seventeenth century. This is not to say, however, that some form of the technique was unknown before then, especially since *muirburn* was a common and comparable operation.

About the year 1662 Gordon of Straloch wrote a description of Aberdeenshire and Banffshire, in which he said that:

> When, several centuries ago, all places were shaggy with woods to the great hindrance of tillage, as these forests were felled, or were rotting with age, moss grew over them, especially in wet and sunken places. The moss was at first light and spongy, but, increasing every year by new additions, grew hard, and became firm and fertile land, which, no doubt, is unfit for the plough unless it is burned, and then the crops luxuriate wonderfully with the ashes. After a year or two new ashes must be had with new fires. Farmers, induced by this store of manure, eagerly desire these lands. The earth itself to a depth of eight, and sometimes twelve feet, is clothed with this layer; but when opened up it discloses huge trunks of trees parted from their roots or rotten with age, and in many instances destroyed by fire (Gordon II (1907), 224, 268).

Another undated but probably seventeenth-century source, relating to the Buchan district of Aberdeenshire, noted that:

> About the Coast side, they make much use of Sea-ware for dunging the Land; in other places they cast Fail (sods) in one piece of ground and lay it on another. And because they have plenty of Moss & Moor; they often car and burn them, and in such burnt Land, they will have incredible increase, 16 or 20 bolls, after one Bolls sowing (Anon. III (1907), 224).

These two sources suggest the existence of two methods. In Gordon of Straloch's account, the moss appears to have been burned on the spot, presumably after some form of cutting and drying, though this is not specified, and indeed is not necessary in deep mosses in dry seasons. In the second account, the turf is cut in one place and carried off for burning and spreading of the ashes in another. This is not paring and burning in the usually accepted sense, but parallels the common practice of cutting turf in moor and meadow land for removal as a means of increasing the amount of domestically produced manure. The making of earth middens, locally called *yirdy tams*, went on at least till the 1860s in parts of Buchan.

The cutting of turf to increase the midden, to use as bedding in the byre, to lay on the roofs of houses by itself or as an underlay for straw thatch, and to build dykes for folding stock, meant that great quantities were required for the everyday functioning of pre-enclosure communities, and since on occasion it seriously reduced the extent of grazing near the houses, there was frequent legislation in the Baron Courts against it. In one Aberdeenshire parish, on 9 May 1664, this practice was roundly denounced along with that of muirburn:

> The said day the haill tenentis underwrittin is fund gultie be the birliemen chossin be thair maister for the pariochin respective, to witt John Leith in Kirktoun of Forbes, Margrett Bonnar thair, the haill tenentis of Baffour, Patrik Jamsone in Sralonack, Alexr. Garvy, John Cleirchew in Putrachie, William Sharp thair, John Geilles, Jean Chalmer, Alexr. Forbes, the haill tenentis of Glentown, for castin ane haill fold, James Duncan and James Clark in Perse low, Alexr. Anderson Stonfeidle, John Lang in Castellhill, George Mackie in Stondyk, and John Glas and Georg Tailzour, for burning murburnes in forbidding tym, the haill abowwrittin persons is fund gultie of casting with foot spades and flachter spades in meadow grownd, hyning, corn land, lones and burning murburne in forbidding tymes, ewry one of them for thair owin pairties is decerned and ordained to pey to thair maister for their faltis the soume of ten poundes for ewry foott spad and fyw pundis for ewry flachter spad, attour [?] ten poundes for ewry murburne, according to former actes (Forbes III (1919), 245-6).

Infringement of the rules was widespread, to judge by the number of individuals referred to. It is also clear that two types of spades were in use, the foot spade and the flauchter spade, the former incurring a heavier fine and therefore capable of doing more damage in meadow lands, probably because of its deeper penetration. On the other hand, a writer in 1729 was more worried by the flauchter spade, presumably because it could clear considerable areas more quickly. After referring to the cutting and carrying home of sods and turf for middens and for thatching, he commented:

> But grant it is a good manure, I think it is a very dear one, to tir [strip] one Area to put upon another; and may be frequently seen in many Places of our Country, nothing but Pebbles and Gravel left a Mile in Circumference in many Estates.

He recommended that landlords should make their tenants draw earth from pits to save the sward, and went on:

But if this Foot-spade and Dunghill be bad, it is nothing to the Flaughter-spade, as we call the Breast-plough for Thatch they make a fearful Havock and Ruin of our best Medow Ground and green Sward; and tho' by our Laws it is strictly defended, that wild Abuse our Nobility and Gentry see it every Day practised at their very Doors, without Concern.

For this ruinous Practice they plead two Reasons; the First is, for thatching their Houses. The Second, as the Foot-spade Feal was for the Dunghill, so this, after coming off their Houses, is better (Mackintosh 1729, 57-8).

This account brings out the distinction between the foot spade and the flauchter spade. The former was used for cutting deep, earthy sods, suitable for chopping up in a midden, the second for cutting shallower turf, suitable for laying on the roofs of houses.

The 'foot spade' is first referred to in the *Acta Dominorum Concilii* in 1489, along with a shovel, and a 'flauchter spade' in the same source in 1493. The two are subsequently mentioned frequently in conjunction with each other, as well as with peat spades, and 'dyk spaidis' (*DOST*, s.v. *flauchter spade, fute-spade*). At least from the fifteenth century there was a variety of spade types, of which at least two were particularly suited for cutting sods and turf, and therefore capable of being used, if desired, in a paring-and-burning technique of cultivation.

The visual evidence for Scottish spade types goes back as far as the seventeenth century, and is found on tombstones. The earliest so far noted is at Abercorn in West Lothian in 1657, and shows a crossed rake and spade with a pointed, asymmetrical blade and an asymmetrical handle on the end of the shaft (Christison 1901-2, 337) (Fig. 20a). Of the same date is a pair of spades shown side by side on the ridge of the roof slab of a coffin from Pittenweem, Fife, one of the same form, and the other with a square-mouthed, symmetrical, straight-shouldered blade and D-handle (*Ib.*, 373) (Fig. 20b). Three stones are Logie Pert, Angus, dated 1664, 1666 and 1667, show a similar pair of spades, crossed, those with symmetrical blades having either square or rounded shoulders (*Ib.*, 304, 306, 308) (Fig. 20c, d, e). The same group occurs at the Port of Menteith, Perthshire, in 1676 (*Ib.*, 39 (1904-5), 64) (Fig. 20f), on an undated stone at Marykirk, Kincardineshire (Fig. 20g), and at Blackford, Perth in 1704 (*Ib.*, 36 (1901-2), 376, 401) (Fig. 20h). A particularly fine pair on the flat tombstone for Alexander Duff of Keithmore in Mortlach Church, Banffshire (Fig. 20i), is so well done and well preserved that the wooden blade shod with iron can be clearly seen on each.

In later examples the form begins to vary somewhat. Thus in 1723 at

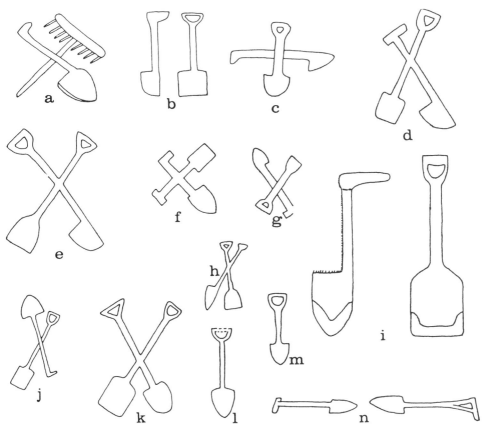

Fig. 20. Representations of spades and shovels on tombstones. (a) Abercorn, 1657; (b) Pittenweem, 1657; (c, d, e) Logie Pert, 1664, 1666, 1667; (f) Port of Menteith, 1676; (g) Marykirk, no date; (h) Blackford, 1704; (i) spade and shovel, Mortlach, 17th century; (j) Haddington, 1723; (k) Inverarity, 1737; (l) Aberfoyle, 1756; (m) Logierait, 1774; (n) flauchter, Glenalmond, probably 18th century, from a photograph, slightly foreshortened.

Haddington, East Lothian, the asymmetrical spade has a pointed, symmetrical blade, though retaining the one-sided handle (*Ib.*, 39 (1904-5), 95) (Fig. 20j), and at Inverarity, Angus, in 1737 the blade is similar and the handle is in the form of a symmetrical, triangular D (*Ib.*, 36 (1901-2), 352) (Fig. 20k). The Tod Monument at Aberfoyle, Perth, 1756 and a stone at Logierait, Perth, 1774 also have pointed symmetrical spades with D-handles (*Ib.*, 39 (1904-5), 59) (Fig. 20l, m).

Since the asymmetrical spade in these examples has a sturdy foot-rest forming part of the top of the blade, it seems reasonable to assume that this is the 'foot spade' of the early records. Though the evidence is

insufficient as a basis for firm conclusions, nevertheless the later forms
in Fig. 20 suggest that it was being modified or replaced in the earlier
part of the eighteenth century. The symmetrical spade that accompanies
it in these illustrations is not a flaughter spade but a shovel. It sometimes has round shoulders and must, therefore, have been thrust in
with the arms alone.

The flaughter spade itself makes only one possible appearance on an
undated but probably eighteenth-century tombstone at Glenalmond,
Perthshire (*Ib.*, 103) (Fig. 20n). Here, there are two spades, with large,
pointed, symmetrical blades, one with a T-handle, and the other with a
forked shaft and crossbar handle reminiscent of one form of the
flaughter spade. Apart from this, the form of the early flaughter spade
can only be ascertained from surviving examples and book illustrations
of comparatively recent date.

Ribbing and Burning

The cutting of turf for burning could be carried out not only by the
spade, however, but also by the plough. In an Aberdeenshire study of
1735, various types and conditions of soil were examined and approp-
riate techniques of cultivation recommended. One type of land was
known as 'laighs', low-lying ground near or among the hills. 'Laighs'
might consist of either 'burnt lands' or 'one fur (furrow) ley', the first
moss-covered, the second having all the moss removed from the
surface. The place-name 'Bruntlands', common in north-east Scotland,
commemorates land of this nature brought or kept under cultivation by
a burning technique.

'Burnt lands' were divided into five classes, (a) 'daichy' (rich,
'doughy') fat soil, to be ploughed and burned before harvest; (b)
'ironory' (impregnated with iron) soil, to be ploughed and burned in
summer and fired again before sowing; (c) a 'stickly' (full of sticks)
moss, to be ribbed, burned, and ploughed in summer; (d) a drossy
deep moss, that encourages the growth of sorrel, to be twice burned;
(e) moss accumulated by wind-blow on hard ground alongside bogs, to
be ribbed and burned in summer. The term 'ribbing' is applied to the
practice of turning the individual furrows right over on their backs to
lie on the unploughed land alongside, rather as is now done by ploughs
drawn by caterpillar tractors during forestry planting (Dodgshon and
Jewell 1970, 82ff).

'*Daichy burnt land*' could be treated in three ways. First, it would be ploughed three times about the middle of the ridge to make it stand high. The third or highest furrow was then set in heaps on the middle. The rest was ploughed, then the heaps were fired, and the ashes covered till sowing time came, when they were spread out, and bere or barley was sown. Second, it could be ribbed with small furrows, and these broken up, heaped, burned, and spread immediately. The field was left till the vegetation cover regenerated before being ploughed for seed. This burning had to be as near harvest as possible. Third, the field could be ploughed up in August or September, and left till March or April before being burned. This was done by using kindlings or combustible turf, cast and prepared the previous summer, set in heaps three or four paces apart on each ridge, kindled, and covered with earth, more earth being added each time fire appeared, until there were enough ashes for the ridge. This is probably the practice alluded to in the seventeenth century by Gordon of Straloch. The bottoms of the heaps were slightly dug. The ground should be left for three years, and should then be ready for a crop of bere (four-rowed barley) or two crops of oats.

'*Ironory land*' was similarly treated. It was burned after being ribbed with small furrows, and again with kindling, before being sown with one crop of bere or two of oats. If it was not burned twice in this way, it would only bear two crops and then had to be left to lie for five years.

'*Stickly moss*', full of old trees, was·ribbed, then burned, preferably with the assistance of a favourable gale of wind, given a shallow ploughing immediately afterwards, and left till seedtime. One crop of 'broak'd corn' (mixed black and white oats) was sown, then the ground was left in grass for two years. Some people burned a second time before sowing, and kept it in corn every second year.

'*Deep moss*'. After having lain for three years, the ground was ribbed in summer, burned, and the unturned ribs were then broken up. Sometimes it was burned and ploughed again. If there was a drought at the time of sowing it would be burned then, and sown and harrowed immediately. One crop of small corn would be taken.

'*Hard ground*'. At the sides of the mosses there was hard ground onto which frosted moss was blown in the spring. After about five years, when it was well swarded with moss, it was ribbed with small, shallow furrows. In a dry season it would run fire, otherwise heaps had to be made and burned in the ordinary way. This took two crops of small corn (Arbuthnot 1735, in Souter 1812, Appx., 83-8).

D

The same procedure of ribbing and burning was also known in Kincardineshire in 1735, where, according to an estate regulation, 'no ground be brunt until after the first of Jully yearly, and non brunt at all except what is ribb'd and above two foot deep of black or moss ground, and that non be over brunt' (Barron 1892, 155). This technique appears to have been very common, for one of the members of the Gordon's Mill Farming Club, a group of agricultural enthusiasts who met for discussion in Aberdeen during the 1750s and 1760s, commented that besides 'tathing' (manuring by the droppings of animals), dunghills, and 'faughing' (a form of outfield fallowing), the chief method of manuring was 'by burning leys, mosses, & draining laights of a mossy quality, burning them also'. In summer, 1750, he observed 'all the country in a smoke'.

Considerable damage could be done when the burning was not sufficiently controlled. It was reported in the *Aberdeen Journal* for September 1748 that the wind 'was so violent that the Burnt land came up upon, and consumed five houses in the Parish of Echt, and several Peat stacks in the moss of Skene'. For this reason, and because of the harm that might be done to the ground, landowners had sometimes to seek help from the courts, as the Earl of Kintore did in 1740.

In 1759, Mr Douglas of Fechil told members of the Gordon's Mill Farming Club that:

> In New Deer & neighbouring parishes the tenants formerly burnt their dry faughs, which were ribbed the beginning of summer, the turf set in heaps kindled, &, when reduced to ashes, spread over the ridges, & plowed in for corn to be sown the following spring; after which three & sometimes four crops were taken. But now, that there is plenty of lime in that corner, the practice is disused.
>
> In the same parishes worn out mosses are still burnt. Careless, unwise fellows rib as above, never set the turf but when it is dry kindle it in several places, by which means if the season proves droughty, attended with wind, the fire runs & spreads in such a manner as to reduce the whole soil to a mass of ashes . . . But the more skilful farmer about the end of May or the beginning of June, with his plough lays 4 furrows together in the middle of every ridge, a part of which he sets up & burns it when dry, carefully covering up the ashes. Before or after the harvest, as most convenient, he plows the ley part of the ridges; & the following spring spreads the ashes & harrows them in with grain. Where their burnt-land[s], as they call them, are deep moss, they take the opportunity of a dry summer, & kindle them in sundry places, when they think there are ashes enough they put out the fire, if they can; but often they cannot. The following spring these ashes are partly spread on the moss itself, which is neither ploughed nor dug before that time. The remainder is carried as manure to other grounds in the neighbourhood. Bear is sown & plentiful crops obtained (Smith 1962, 72, 110-2).

By the end of the eighteenth century, the practice had almost died out. In 1794 the laigh-lands were described as

> . . . a kind of low lying moist meadow ground, sometimes with a mixture of moss. They are invariably plowed three years for oats on one furrow, and are allowed to be in grass for three years, and so on alternately without ever receiving any dung. Brunt-lands are now very generally managed after the same manner. These are always of a mossy nature. The turf when broke up from grass used to be gathered into heaps and burnt, and immediately sown with bear, after which two crops of oats were taken in succession, and then it was suffered to run to grass. But this practice of burning having been found prejudicial is now very generally prohibited, so that the practice is rare, though the patches that had been formerly subjected to it still retain that name (Anderson 1794, 54-7).

By 1811, ribbing and burning had gone more or less completely out of use for fertilising 'burnt lands' (Keith 1811, 429-30).

Information on this technique, which may be described as 'ribbing and burning', to distinguish it from 'paring and burning' with the spade, is rare elsewhere, but occurred, for example, in Dunbartonshire and in Galloway where it was formerly much practised for breaking up the moors in some areas. After ploughing, the turf was collected in heaps and burnt during the summer. Three or four oat crops were subsequently taken and over-cropping, along with total lack of dung, reduced the soil to 'a mere *caput mortuum*'. Many landlords prohibited this practice and several tenants gave it up of their own free will (Whyte and Macfarlan 1811, 188; Smith 1810, 222-3).

An account of the 1790s, for Carnwarth, Lanarkshire, shows that the method there was similar:

> In the mossy lands there is a peculiar mode of cultivation observed. When the moss is deep, and so soft as not to bear the plough horses in winter, it is sometimes ploughed in the drought of summer; burnt when so dry as to burn, the ashes spread over the whole, and then sown down in spring, without any further cultivation, with barley and oats; and in favourable seasons a very rich crop is produced. Moss, of this kind, repeatedly burnt, becomes thinner and thinner, till it disappears almost or altogether, and leaves the clay, that was once three or four feet down, on the surface. Some hundreds of acres have been converted in this manner from moss to make arable land (*OSA* X (1794), 328).

In the north, the practice was also known in Nairn and Moray, as an extension of the technique of 'brake-furrowing', done in the autumn as a substitute for winter fallow. This was the same as ribbing, and the term 'brak-fur', 'to half-plough in such a way as to lay the up-turned furrow over the uncut furrow', or, as a noun, a kind of half-ploughing, or cross-ploughing in autumn, was remembered in Banffshire and Morayshire into the late 1930s (*SND*, s.v.). It was done there for ground previously in cultivation that was to be broken up from grass. The turf was collected in heaps, dried a little, and burned. Then the whole area was ploughed and a good crop of barley, followed by one of oats, was obtained. About fifty or sixty acres were worked in this way annually (Leslie 1811, 141-2, 279-80).

Though this is not quite the same as the ribbing of peaty ground, nevertheless it is clearly the same technique, and the distribution of ribbing and burning, from Moray to Galloway, must suggest a formerly fairly wide distribution.

In ribbing and burning, the main tool was the plough, but two points must be made in order to see the technique in perspective. Firstly, the spade was not an integral element, though it was almost certainly used in breaking the cast-up rib or furrow into manageable pieces, after the ploughing had been done. Second, the plough used was the ordinary four-sided one, not a special paring plough with a broad share and vertical wing adapted for cutting shallow slices of turf. These only came into use in the latter part of the eighteenth century in England, for example in Cheshire (Dickson I (1805), Plate L), and in the first half of the nineteenth century the Agricultural Museum of the Highland and Agricultural Society of Scotland contained a paring plough model (*Catalogue* 1841, 16) presented by Sir C. G. S. Menteith, of Dumfriesshire, in 1840. Though used successfully (Rennie, in Sinclair II (1814), 408), there is nevertheless no evidence that such ploughs functioned in Scotland on a scale that would give them significance in the development of Scottish agriculture. Even in the mid-nineteenth century the plough called a 'ribbing or paring plough' was not a special type, but an ordinary, small-sized iron plough, capable of making ribs as narrow as 9 in. (22.9 cm.) (Stephens II (1844), 501, Fig. 370). A corollary to this is the fact that ribbing was not necessarily followed by burning. It was merely that burning happened to answer best as a means of dealing with peaty, low-lying ground. Ribbing survived into the nineteenth century without the accompaniment of burning and was described in the following terms by a writer of 1844:

> I notice it, because it is practised in some parts, not with the view of recom-
> mending but of reprobating it. It is, I believe, called *raftering* in England, and is
> practised on stubble land, and consists of laying a furrow-slice on its back upon as
> much of the firm soil as it can cover . . . It is sometimes ploughed so as the furrow-

slice shall lap and hand over the piece of firm soil upon which it rests and the plough-tracks are often very crooked. The land lies in this state all winter, and is dry enough; but the greatest proportion of the soil remaining unploughed, is none the better for this treatment. It has the advantage of being done in a short time, and without care, as it is generally done in a diagonal direction across the ridges, and without any sort of feering (a furrow drawn to mark out plough ridges). It is chiefly practised on land in a very foul state, with the view of destroying the weeds; it is practised in all sorts of soils. Its practice in Scotland is confined to the north of the Firth of Forth, and even there is now abandoned on the large farms, though it may still be seen in the fields of the smaller tenants (*Ib.*, I, 481-2).

Here is the end of a long tradition that goes back at least to the seventeenth century in so far as it was linked with burning, and in the north-east of Scotland in particular the ribbing and burning technique seems to have been firmly entrenched even then. There are also variations in the method to be noted: the cutting of turf with the foot or flauchter spade to be transported to another place for burning, the heaping and burning of the surface of a moss by a running fire, without paring. The fact of such variety, indicating adaptation to local or climatic conditions, suggests a well-established tradition. In its social background as well as in its methods, it is very different from the paring and burning that developed as an adjunct to reclamation on big estates in the late eighteenth and nineteenth centuries, often as a follow-up to the enclosure of common land.

Paring and Burning

The Lothians and the Border Counties appear to have been amongst the earliest to apply paring and burning to reclamation. On John Cockburn's estate at Ormiston in East Lothian, improvements in the first half of the eighteenth century included:

> . . . the surface levelled; ridges properly formed, and directed to carry off moisture; drains made in wet places; summer-fallowing; lime; clay burnt into ashes, and spread on grass or fallow; pairing and burning coarse land, inclined to clay, and spreading the ashes; moderate corn-crops, and frequent grass-crops from seed sown (Wight II (1778), 136).

In 1805, paring and burning was almost unknown in East Lothian. It was said to have been tried without much success, partly because the labourers were not acquainted with the process, and could neither do it well nor on moderate terms (Somerville 1805, 174-5). There is no reference to it in the earlier report of 1794 on the agriculture of East Lothian.

In Berwickshire it had already disappeared by 1809, having been used as a stimulant to coarse, grassy lands during a scourging form of cropping and not for permanent improvement (Kerr 1809, 210, 363). Nevertheless, only a few years before, in 1797, it had been described as a novelty in the county (Home 1794, 98).

In Roxburgh, 'some years ago, huge crops were raised by paring and burning, to the great emolument of the tenants, but much to the prejudice of their farms and their successors'. In Selkirk it had never been general and appeared to have been completely given up by 1813, and indeed already by 1794, though still going on in the adjoining county of Teviotdale (Douglas 1813, 132, 191; Johnston 1794, 33-4).

In Dumfriesshire, Sir William Maxwell of Springkell improved his 450-acre farm, after 1761, by draining, paring and burning, and liming. Presumably with his support, or at his instigation, one John James left the job of Excise Officer in England to cultivate moss on the estate. He brought 'a profusion of spades, hoes, rakes, &c. of many different shapes and sizes; but the only excellence I could discover in them was, that they were agreeable to the fancy of the owner, and afforded him an opportunity of laughing at the clumsy tools used in Dumfriesshire'. By 1811 his tools were rusting away and the native tools were still in active use (Wight II (1778), 433; Aiton 1811, 205). In the 1790s, paring and burning was referred to in the parishes of Leswalt, Inch, and Whithorn in Wigtonshire, and Twynholm in Kirkcudbrightshire (*OSA* III (1792), 135, 318-9; XVI (1795), 281; XV (1795), 83), not always in favourable terms. The Twynholm account said that paring and burning was in general the worst husbandry, except on deep mossy ground with a clay bottom. In Whithorn it had already died out, and the practice was alleged to be now 'everywhere reprobated in Galloway'. In Leswalt, cultivation had been successfully carried out by paring (here called 'ripping', perhaps with reference to the action of the upright wing. of the breast spade) and burning the sod. After spreading the ashes, seven or eight crops of oats, or more, had been taken, and some farms had done this with success three times on the same ground. Afterwards, it was noted, the grass degenerated, and became very coarse, like bent.

In Dumfries, in 1794, paring and burning was not much esteemed or practised, least of all on shallow soils that were hard to drain, though in 1812 one writer thought it was not so much practised in the county as it ought to be, provided it was applied in the right conditions. He noted that very few labourers made paring their business (as was the case in England), and that the cost of the operation, including the spreading of the ashes, was about £2 per acre. An improver specifically mentioned was Mr Menteath of Closeburn, who had reclaimed mossy moors by paring and burning, then by ploughing not more than 3 in. (7.6 cm.) deep, and liming, and sowing out with grasses, not grain crops (Johnston 1794, 64-5; Singer 1812, 65, 321-3).

In Galloway, in 1811, paring and burning had lately been in use in several places, though rarely on bogs or flow mosses where the surface was very uneven. When these were pared, some of the turf was used to fill up the hollows. The rest was collected into heaps, or built into 'kilns', and burned. The flame should not be allowed to burst out during the process. The ashes were scattered as powder, the moss was dug by the spade to a depth of a few inches, and a crop of bere, barley, or potato oats sown the following spring. Paring was done with spades of two types. One was an ordinary spade, rounded in the mouth and sharpened from time to time. The other was a so-called flaying, paring or flauchter spade, with a steeled face, with which the work could be done more quickly. Its blade was 8-9 in. (20-23 cm.) broad by 3-4 in. (7.6-10 cm.) deep, the neck 2-4 in. (5-10 cm.) broad, and slightly angled, strong enough to stand the strain of raising the turf, the shaft 4 ft. (122 cm.) long, or sometimes 6-7 ft. (183-213 cm.) long, in which case the bend at the neck was shallower. One side of the blade had a vertical wing that cut the turf like the coulter of a plough, and the user protected his thighs by wooden plates attached to his body. Paring and burning was found to work best, however, on bogs consisting of peat mixed with alluvial soil or common earth, and the ashes would produce enough manure at a time for two or three successive crops. Sir Alexander Gordon was the first to practise it extensively on land banked from the River Dee. He divided the bog into fields of three to four acres by ditches, allowing them to drain sufficiently to take the weight of a plough in dry weather. The furrows were cut up, built into kilns, burned, and the ashes scattered immediately, and ploughed in as soon as convenient. Crops of oats and barley, several in succession, were followed by turnips and potatoes. Sown grasses also did very well. The influence of England is apparent here since Sir Alexander's improvements were based on his observation of the method practised in Berkshire. Mr Cathcart of Genoch tried the same process, though burning his furrows on the field without first stacking them in heaps, and he proposed to sow rape-seed, a new crop for Galloway. By contrast Mr Craik of Arbigland, a well-known agriculturist, experimented with paring and burning on a poorly drained area and succeeded in destroying the peaty surface, so that the soil was worse after than it had been before (Smith 1810, 222-7).

The writer of the agricultural survey of Ayrshire in 1811 noted that

> . . . paring and burning, so common in some parts of England, and so much praised by some of their writers on agriculture, have been sometimes tried, but seldom approved of in Scotland. Those operations have been attempted in Ayrshire, but are now altogether abandoned, and detested in that district (Aiton (a) II (1811), 373).

In the Middle Ward of Clydesdale, John Naismith reported the successful paring and burning of bogs using a subsequent top-dressing of lime, sand, gravel, and clay (Naismith (1798), 1806, 103-4).

In Renfrewshire, in 1812, paring and burning was not done, but straight burning of the mosses and moors sometimes took place. The former was for reclamation, by mixing the ashes and moss with what remained of the subsoil. The moor burning was to encourage the growth of grass (Wilson 1812, 132). Boyd Alexander, M.P., reclaimed bog in Renfrewshire in 1803 by digging with the spade and manuring with dung and lime (Steele 1826, 63).

In Dunbarton, in 1811, paring and burning was practised, though not as commonly as it appeared to have been earlier. After most of the peat had been dug for fuel in the flat mosses around Kirkintilloch, Cumbernauld, and Kilmarnock, the remaining small amount of peat was often burned, together with part of the clayey subsoil. The ashes were spread immediately and ploughed down, giving tolerable crops, but this practice was not widespread. The main use for paring and burning was in reclaiming waste lands and in breaking up old pastures on the edges of moors, where these had become overrun with coarse grasses, heath, furze, and rushes. Two good crops could be grown, and the pasture left in an improved state. In such situations the soil was thin, and was seldom pared and burned till it had lain twelve to twenty years in pasture, since repeated paring and burning was regarded as harmful by diminishing the vegetable content of the soil. The depth pared seldom exceeded 1½ in. (3.8 cm.), and was done by the 'breast or flauchter spade'. In some cases, land to be burned was given two ribbings by the common plough, but this was comparatively rare. The turf was collected in small heaps and burned as slowly as possible, the ashes were spread when cool, and lime was usually applied a few days later; this normally took place in July. However, the technique did not play any great part in the total economy of the county (Whyte and Macfarlan 1811, 187-9).

In Fife, in 1800, it had only been tried in a few instances, on newly drained fenny ground, or on land with a mossy surface. It was not recommended, except where other manure was absolutely lacking (Thomson 1800, 238-40). In 1802, Thomas Kinnear of Kinloch, Fife improved a deep peat moss by draining, levelling and burning, using a common spade. The ashes were spread ½ in. (1.3 cm.) thick, mixed with the peat soil to prevent blowing. This moss could bear a plough and horses the second year after draining. James Kinnear, farmer at Lordscairnie in Fife, improved forty-seven acres of bog by draining, ploughing a year later, and burning the furrow slices. This gave him a good turnip crop. James Gordon of Culvennan, a Director of the Highland and Agricultural Society of Scotland, improved one hundred acres in Galloway in the same way. In using the plough, both of these gentlemen were imitating, perhaps unconsciously, the practice of earlier generations. Captain Cheape of Rossie, Fife used the ordinary 'flaughter spade' for paring (Steele 1826, 32, 54-80).

In Kinross, in 1814, paring and burning was done only on moss, for an oat crop (Graham 1814, 124).

In Stirling, in 1796, peat earth was burned in the neighbourhood of the mosses, and the ashes were spread on the ground as a top-dressing. This was practised only by the poorest farmers; it had been much in use on the shallow outskirts of mosses at Buchlyvie, Kippen, and Gargunnock, but by 1812 it had almost ceased (Belsches 1796, 39; Graham 1812, 198, 249).

In Perth, in 1799, paring and burning was practised less than in former years, and had rarely or never been in use in the eastern districts. Some farmers, however, were interested enough to have asked the Board of Agriculture to send a person skilled in the subject to various parts of the county, to point out the soils best suited for it, and to instruct them in the technique (Robertson 1799, 274-5). In 1794, it was said that in the southern districts of Perth, small mosses, where there was a good mixture of other earth, and where the ground was sloping, were generally pared and burned with profit. If the moss was fairly level, however, it was planted with potatoes in lazybeds. Deep mosses with plenty of brushwood were drained, and then pared and burned. According to James Robertson,

> . . . the spade for *paring* ought to be similar to that used in Scotland for casting
> turf, only a little more scooped in the iron and rounder in the fore part, with a
> perpendicular knife at one side of the iron, to cut the peat, as the Highland people
> have to the *lugged* spade, which they sometimes use for casting peats in tough
> mosses (Robertson 1794, 98-9).

In Angus, in 1813, paring and burning had never been practised,
though Mr Drocket, farmer at Flemington, near Aberlemno, used an
equivalent form to improve a field of waste land. He first ploughed
with a shallow furrow, then cross-ploughed to cut up the furrow slices.
These clods were dried and carted home for use as fuel in his kitchen
and outhouses. The resultant ashes were carefully kept and spread over
the field which in the meantime had had a winter and spring fallow.
Potatoes and turnips were sown, and thereafter the field was brought
under the same rotation as the rest of the farm. Though harking back
to a method well known at an earlier period, this was an 'uncommon
. . . mode of conducting this process, and . . . laughed at while it was
going on'. It proved successful, but was not imitated (Headrick 1813,
383, 396).

In Aberdeenshire, in 1811, paring and burning was little practised
and in most cases expressly forbidden. Where dung could not be had,
however, 'it was doubted [i.e. considered] by many, whether paring off
one or two inches with the breast plough, (provincially, *casting thin
flaughter feal*) would not be beneficial', provided turnips followed, and
the land had been drained in advance. Bere or oats, with sown grasses,
should succeed the turnips. The process should not be repeated on the
same land (Keith 1811, 429-30). Clearly, the technique was a novelty
here.

In Nairn and Moray, in 1811, in the new settlements established on
the edges of the mountains or in some of the valleys, partly resulting
from clearance of the old settlement areas for sheep grazing,

> . . . the poor people sometimes improve a small plot of moorish ground
> immediately from the waste, by cutting up the surface into turf by a particular
> spade in a semi-lunular form, with a long head upon the top of the shaft, by which
> it is pushed underneath the surface by the power of the arms, assisted by the
> pressure of the thighs of the man who works it. In this county it is known by the
> name of the *Flaughter*, as if the *flaying* spade, and it is principally used for cutting
> up the thin sods for thatching houses. The turf thus flayed off and dryed a little, is
> imperfectly burned, and the ground ploughed once; a scanty and unequal crop,
> generally of barley, is obtained (Leslie 1811, 279).

In Inverness, in 1808, paring and burning was confined to one or two improvers like Mr Fraser of Achnagairn, in the parish of Kirkhill. He got a good yield of wheat from fifteen acres pared and burned on his farm of Grome (Robertson 1808, 231-2).

In Sutherland, the story was the same, apart from one or two spots such as a peat bog at Clyne, where the tenant, Major Houston, had four acres pared and burned in 1806. He collected the pared material in a nearby gravel pit, burned it there, and mixed it with sea-sand before spreading it (Henderson 1812, 92).

In Caithness also there was no tradition of treating land in this way except amongst the gentry. Mr Innes of Isault improved twenty acres of moss ground at a cost of thirty shillings per acre, taking one crop of oats sown with grass-seed, and then leaving it in pasture for several years. In 1802 Sir John Sinclair imported five men from Westmorland, accustomed to paring with the breast spade. They pared eighty acres of green common on his property in one season, starting in April, and then the ground was enclosed with a ditch and laid out in four equal fields. The sods were burned and the ashes spread by the end of July, and lightly ploughed in for a crop of turnip and cabbage. In 1803 the same five or possibly three (Sinclair, in Steele 1826, 331) men pared seventy acres in the hills of Thurso East and Skinnet. The sods were burned that season, but the ashes kept till April 1804 before being spread. They gave a good crop of red oats that nearly covered the cost of paring and burning, and enclosing with a ditch. The Westmorland breast spade pared a sod 1-2 in. (2.5-5 cm.) thick.

Amongst others who had improved commons by this method were James Troull of Hobbister on his property in the parishes of Dunnet and Olrig, and the Earl of Caithness on the estate of Mey. Some of these improved areas were then let out in small lots of from three to twelve acres to fishermen and crofters (Henderson 1812, 172-9).

The breast spade used by Sir John Sinclair's imported Westmorland workmen was an innovation in Caithness, where the native implement for paring turf was the flauchter spade. A type of paring plough from the Cambridgeshire fens, with labourers from the same area, was also tried in the Ord of Caithness (Aiton (b) 1811, 205, 312).

Though the main phase of paring and burning in Scotland was in the late eighteenth and early nineteenth centuries, it continued far into the nineteenth century. In New Cumnock, Ayrshire, in the 1840s, paring and burning was followed by liming. On Sir C. G. S. Menteath's estate at Closeburn, Dumfriesshire, where it was done on dry moors with a sandy subsoil, no heather had reappeared in the course of twenty years in some cases (*NSA* V (1845), 519). In Lochmaben, Dumfriesshire, the cutting or paring of peat moss, and burning it, before a crop of oats, was described as a modern improvement in the 1840s (*NSA* IV (1845), 390). By this time, however, it was becoming rarer, and, significantly, was not discussed in the first edition of H. Stephens' *Book of the Farm* in 1844, implying that it was a matter of little importance. The next edition of 1855 (and its Swedish translation of 1858) does, however, incorporate a full description and an illustration of the breast spade, though this was more applicable to England (and Sweden) than to Scotland, where the flauchter spade was the indigenous tool.

Enough had been said to show that Professor David Low, holder of the first Chair in Agriculture at Edinburgh University, was not quite accurate when he said in 1834 that paring and burning was unknown in Scotland (and the North of England) (Low 1834, 178). His statement does indicate, however, that the technique was of little significance. Between about 1760 and 1820, numerous landlords had used paring and burning as a means of reclamation, from Galloway to Caithness, sometimes using English workers and sometimes the long-handled English breast spade with a vertical wing on the blade. But this task tended to be a once and for all affair, after which the reclaimed area was fitted into the general farming rotation. There is little or no evidence that paring and burning played any part in rotational sequences in Scotland, as it did in parts of England like Hampshire, where it might take place in any one area about every ten, twelve, or fourteen years, though since 'raftering' (that is, ribbing) was also done there when the soil was too flinty for the breast spade, it is conceivable that such rotational burning has a tradition behind it similar to that of ribbing and burning in Scotland (Driver 1794, 68).

In Scotland, paring and burning associated with the breast spade or flauchter spade scarcely antedates the mid-eighteenth century. In England it has a much longer tradition, particularly in the south-west where there may have been an extension of the practice in the late sixteenth and early seventeenth centuries, when large tracts of the moorlands of Devon and Cornwall were made fertile by sand, seaweed, marl, lime, soap ashes, and paring and burning, under the impetus of expanding markets and rising population. In the 1620s the free commoners of Dartmoor were taking in farms from the moors by paring and burning, and in the 1690s it was being done on the shoulders of Plynlimon in central Wales, at a height of 1000 ft (Thirsk

1967, 76, 116). It was probably during this period of expansion that the breast spade developed in its standard form with a long shaft, cross-bar handle, and winged metal blade, replacing the system of paring and burning with mattocks in south-west England (Dodgshon and Jewell 1970, 75-7), and also recorded in Wales and Ireland. The breast spade was first referred to under the term 'breast plough' in J. Worlidge's *Systema Agriculturae* of 1609. It is not represented in Walter Blith's *English Improver Improved* of 1653, though the illustrations include an iron-shod wooden turfing spade, and a paring spade with a splayed-out blade. His trenching spade, however, does have two upright wings, from which the idea for the wing of the breast spade may have come. The instrument was first recognisably described by Robert Plot in his *Natural History of Staffordshire* (1686) under the name 'push-plough', and was illustrated in J. Mortimer's *Whole Art of Husbandry* (1721). It was only during the eighteenth century and into the nineteenth (Fussell 1933, 109-14) that the instrument really took a widespread hold, in the course of the enormous amount of reclamation of downland, moor, and commons that took place at that period. In this phase its main use was in initiating the work of reclamation, so that by the end of the eighteenth century there were districts where it was already obsolete — including Devon — partly because it had served its purpose, and partly because its misuse had led to its prohibition by landlords. This was a phase of estate improvement, under which the breast spade and the paring-and-burning technique also spread into Scotland, by direct import of workers and tools, as in Caithness, or through the observation of the practice by Scots lairds in England, or by study of the copious literature that was circulating in the latter half of the eighteenth century.

Because of its rapid spread, the breast spade had very much the same form throughout England, and in the areas to which it penetrated in Scotland and Ireland. In the latter two countries, however, it did not catch on outside estates, no doubt because a locally older and perfectly adequate tool, the flauchter spade, was in everyday use, and perhaps because it was not so easy as in England to get labourers, unused to a new instrument, to hire themselves out as professional parers and burners, except in a few cases in certain areas, like the Carnwath district of Lanarkshire, where the workmen were so expert that they were employed to pare and burn moor ground in other counties (Jackson 1850, 49).

Paring and Burning with the Mattock

This technique, common in parts of Ireland, was rare in Scotland, and only one source has so far been found:

> Where heath is too short to burn standing, it may be very quickly torn up by means of an instrument called by the country people, a cabbir, which is a half pick with a broad end (Mackenzie 1810, 208).

This name is simply the Gaelic word *caibe* (mattock).

Part III
Turf and Peat

5
The Cutting of Turf and Peat

The Flauchter Spade and the Cutting of Turf

The flauchter spade, first referred to in 1493, has had a good five hundred years of active life in Scotland. Though on present evidence the term 'flauchter spade' goes back to the fifteenth century, the fact of turf cutting, requiring some kind of cutting implement, is much older, and the use of turf to supplement the fertility of the infield, either directly applied with or without burning, or after serving as roofing thatch, as bedding in the byre, as earthen dykes and walls of buildings, and as domestic fuel, must be a practice of greater antiquity. Indeed in the north-west German, Dutch, and Danish 'Geest' (arable, sandy soils), sods cut from the heath were used for so long as byre litter and manure that the soil surface around the settlement areas has risen considerably, and radiocarbon dating of the lowest levels takes the practice back to the third to first century B.C. (Uhlig 1961, 189). A striking example of the wholesale removal of peat and turf from the moor to the infields is the small Shetland island of Papa Stour, where two-thirds of the island's area outside the hill dyke have been pared to the bare rocks and stones, and the soil of the settlement third has been deepened considerably as a result.

The two commonest Scottish names for turf that has been cut are 'divot' and 'fail'. 'Divot' is a term of uncertain etymology confined to Scotland and the north of England. It occurs in the records in various forms, such as 'divot', 'devat', 'diffat', 'duvat(e)', of which the last is the earliest, going back to 1435 when it was referred to as building material for Inverness Castle: '*cooperiri faciant cum dwvate tres turres castri*' (Burnett IV (1880), 634). In the Arbroath area in 1456, the 'casting off petis faile na dwuate no nane othir thing that mai rede the erde or skaith the pasture' (cutting of peats, fail nor divots nor any other thing that may remove the earth or harm the pasture), was forbidden (*Liber* II (1856), 89). The majority of references indicate that 'divots' were used for building purposes, and especially for roofing. Enormous quantities were used in this way, and even a modest

Aberdeenshire manse in 1714 had 4000 divots on its roof (Mair 1894, 233-4). A manuscript receipt of 1724 from Fife reads:

> I John Melville in Leslie Grant me to have receaved from William Hay factor to the Earle of Rothes the somme of ten shillings sterling for casting and winning [drying] ten thousand Divotts in the parks of Leslie for the use of the said Earle which is hereby Discharged as witness my hand att Leslie the twintie second day of June 1724 years (Rothes MSS).

Clearly, although estate legislation in many parts of the county had long before this been seeking to control the extent of turf cutting, turf was of such importance in the economy that even the estate owners could not dispense with it until its need was obviated by the extensive use of lime on the fields, and the use of slates and pantiles on roofs.

The term 'fail' is a little older, going back to Wyntoun's *Orygynale Cronykil of Scotland*, c. 1420. In the MS Accounts of the Lord High Treasurer of Scotland for 1472, there is a reference to 'faill castaris for certaine thowsandis faill casting' (*DOST* s.v. *Fail*), and in 1704 the Burgh of Peebles

> ordaines all faill middings, or faill brought in and laid upon the streets, to be removed against Saturdayes night, and discharges the bringing in and laying doune of any more upon the streets, under the penalty of five merks, with libertie to all that pleases to lead them after the same tyme (*Extracts*, 1910, 172).

'Fail' was chiefly used in building walls and dykes, and in making earth middens, and was thicker and earthier than 'divot'. Although the name is found in Gaelic as *fál*, it is likely that the term is a borrowing into Gaelic from Scots, since there is no Irish equivalent. Though 'fail' was probably cut with the 'foot-spade', the flauchter was certainly also used for this purpose and the term 'flauchter-fail' is very common.

It has been estimated that at the present day, about one tenth of the land surface of Scotland is covered by peat-bog, of which 1,700,000 acres (688,500 hectares) are 2 ft. (61 cm.) deep or more (*Peat Surveys* 1964). At the same time, nature was not always kind enough to place these massive reserves of fuel in areas where they were readily available for domestic consumption. Throughout the historical period it is clear that settlement has to a great extent been conditioned by the availability of fuel and that the wearing out of peat supplies was a constant source of difficulty, aggravated for certain places and social classes by the intensification of bog and moorland reclamation that formed part of the eighteenth-century agricultural improvements. Paring and burning

then, and ribbing and burning at an earlier period, along with the
regular annual cutting of peat for fuel, have cleared untold thousands of
acres in the course of centuries, and human activity in the last few
hundred years has led to a general slowing down or complete cessation
of bog regeneration. Burning techniques in particular have a strong
effect on bogs, and if repeated at short intervals lead to a drastic and
apparently irreversible reduction in their cover. Peat cutting itself, as
well as draining, also dries out bogs by lowering the water table
(Burnett 1964, 452-8).

By reason of the wearing out of peat-bogs, and because in many
districts peat was lacking in any case, other materials had to be used for
fuel and of these, until coal came into general use, turf was the most
common. This was the subject of comment by travellers in areas like
the moors after Ayton on the road between Berwick and Edinburgh in
1636:

> Here is a mighty want of fire in these moors; neither coal, nor wood, nor turf
> [peat]; only they cut and flea top-turves with linge [heather] upon them (Brereton,
> in Brown 1891, 134).

From the *Old Statistical Account* and the agricultural surveys of the
1790s, it can be seen that in most Scottish counties several parishes
used turf for fuel, sometimes alongside peat, and sometimes alone. As
peat became scarcer, turf came more into use for fuel, for example in
the parish of Kirkhill, Inverness (*OSA* IX (1792), 113). Parishes with
no indigenous peat and turf had to bring both in from neighbouring
areas, like Logie-Buchan, Aberdeenshire in the 1840s (*NSA* XII
(1845), 816), the Orkney island of Graemsay in the 1790s, which got
fuel from Hoy and other places (*OSA* XVI (1795), 249), and the Ross-
shire parish of Kirkmichael, where

> . . . as there has been no moss in this parish for near a century past; the men and
> horses have been constantly employed, during summer, in cutting, drying, and
> carrying home sandy turfs, or divots, from the Mull-bui, which, at best, is but a
> wretched kind of fuel (*OSA* XIV (1795), 91 footnote).

There are numerous examples of both geographical and social
differentiation. Where there was access to the coast and to sea-ports,
coal could be got and was used in the immediate hinterland but not in
the inland or higher-lying parts. This was the case in Banffshire,
Kirkcudbrightshire and elsewhere till well into the nineteenth century
(Souter 1812, 276-7; *NSA* IV (1845), 96). The extension of the road

system allowed coal to penetrate farther into such areas, however, so that already in the 1790s, coal from Edinburgh and Dalkeith almost entirely supplanted the former use of peat and turf in the Berwick-shire parish of Lauder, after the roads were made (*OSA* I (1791), 77). Here, as in most other places, the use of peat and turf for fuel sank in the social scale to become the fuel of labourers and the poorer classes generally. Coal was sometimes forced on all classes in areas where peat and turf did not exist or had been converted into arable, for example in Kirkmaiden, Wigtownshire (*Ib.*, 157), and in this case the very poor were obliged to glean their 'elding' (firing) any way they could, from materials like sticks, gorse and broom bushes, and docken stalks, enough to cook food, but not to provide constant warmth. Such folk would not stay long if an opportunity arose to move nearer a regular source of fuel, and accounts tell of how farm workers, for instance, built their huts on the moor in Kilmuir-Easter, Ross-shire, so as to be near peats and turf (*OSA* VI (1792), 186). The importance of a fuel supply in relation to questions of settlement patterns and depopulation before about 1850 can scarcely be overestimated.

A major factor in the decline of turf cutting was the influence of estate legislation. In Kincardineshire, in 1604, tenants were forbidden to cut and sell turf, peat, and heather to the inhabitants of the town of Stonehaven, and each husbandman was to be answerable for his servants' obedience (Barron 1892, 4). This was to regulate the excessive enthusiasm of the tenants, however, and was not as final as the edicts that followed division and enclosure of the commons, and agricultural improvements. Peat and turf cutting ceased in Bunkle and Preston, Berwickshire, after improvements began (*OSA* III (1792), 157), and as in Coldingham in the same county, the division of the common led to the general use of coal from Northumberland (*OSA* XII (1794), 44). In Roxburgh parish, all casting of turf on the moors was prohibited some years before 1790 (*OSA* XIX (1797), 129). In Speymouth the division of the moor of Garmouth cut off the local supplies of turf in the early 1800s (*NSA* XIII (1845), 56), and in the parish of Monedie, Perthshire, the paring of ground for turf was similarly forbidden by the proprietors (*OSA* III (1792), 274). The situation whereby a Perthshire minister had carriages for 54 loads of turf and 120 loads of peat as part of his stipend came to an end (*OSA* X (1794), 613). Parallel instances could be multiplied, but in the areas of improved agriculture, particularly in the south and east of Scotland, turf cutting for fuel was rapidly dying out by about 1800, and the dictum of the minister of Carstairs, Lanarkshire, that 'the great obstruction to improvement is the absurd custom of using turf for fuel' (*OSA* XVIII (1796), 177), was reversed.

Turf for fuel had a much higher content of earth or clay than peat, and for this reason it could sometimes be used in a particular way. Frequently a large turf cut with the flauchter spade was set up at the back of the peat fire and in this position burned slowly and threw out a good deal of heat (Walker 2 (1803), 117). In the Northern Isles this was called a 'back-peat' and, in the west, a *tobhtag* or *culag* (Macdonald 29 (1915), 46). Because of the earthy content, the quantity of ash produced was much greater than for ordinary peat, and so in parishes such as Firth and Stenness in Orkney, turf was deliberately pared from moors where there was some admixture of the peat moss with grit or clay, and burned with a few peats to increase the quantity of ashes available for manure (*OSA* XIV (1795), 127; Fenton 1981, 210-17).

In Killearn parish, Stirlingshire, a combination of moorburn and the cutting of turf for fuel obtained. About June, the surface grass and heath was burned, and then the surface was taken up with the flauchter spade (*OSA* XVI (1795), 120). Although there is little evidence one way or the other, it is likely that at least a proportion — perhaps, indeed, the greater proportion — of moorburn in earlier times was not to improve the grazing, but simply to prepare the surface to facilitate the cutting of turf for fuel or any other desired purpose.

With this background in mind, the next stage is to examine the implements regionally used for cutting turf. The earliest description of a flauchter spade is probably the one with a forked shaft and a pointed, half-oval blade, on the undated tombstone referred to above (Fig. 20n). The next was published in 1812 (Fig. 21a) and has a straight shaft with a crescentic blade and stout cross-bar handle. It was described as:

> . . . a divot-spade, *i.e.* a breast spade for casting or cutting divots, or thin sods for thatch to their houses. The metal part of the spade has a semicircular edge, and a socket to receive the wooden handle, about four feet and a half [137 cm.] long, and a little bent, having a cross wooden head; the workman, by pressing his belly to this head, pushes the spade into the ground, nearly in a horizontal direction, in order to cut the sods thin . . . The mouth, or edge of this spade is steeled, and kept very sharp. A man, having a sheep's skin tied round his waist, will earn from 2*s.* to 2*s.* 6*d.* per day, by casting divots with this spade, at the rate of 8*s.* for every 1000 divots (Leslie 1811, 279).

The form matches the description given above (page 98) of a flauchter spade from Nairn and Moray, of 'semilunular form, with a long head upon the top of the shaft', used by poor people in improving patches of

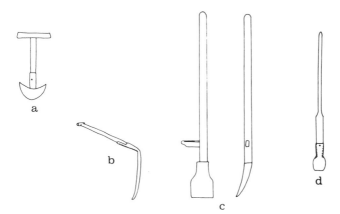

Fig. 21. (a) Flauchter, Caithness, after Henderson 1812; (b) ripper, Orkney; (c) delving spade, Shetland, after Shirreff 1814; (d) moor spade, Shetland. Not to scale.

moor ground. These two forms with straight and forked shafts, and with crescentic or pointed blades, and sometimes heart-shaped blades, represent the usual Scottish types. From the typological point of view, however, the areas that stand out conspicuously are Shetland and Orkney, where two distinct kinds of turf spades are found, as well as a type of knife-shaped turf cutter.

Shetland

The turf cutter is used in the process of 'flaying' or slicing off the surface turf overlying a peat bank, and is a tool of comparatively recent introduction, probably not much if at all before the beginning of this century, also used in Orkney and parts of the Hebrides and Highlands. It is called a 'ripper', 'ritting knife', or 'hack spade' (Fig. 21b) and has been described as 'of the shape of a jet of gas from an ordinary burner with a slight curve forward, so that the cutting is done slantwise' (Leask I.iv (1907), 134). It has a wooden handle on the end of which a long, knife-like blade is fixed at an angle of about one hundred degrees, with its front side sharpened so that it can cut by being thrust forward, in a series of slicing motions. Its purpose is to cut a slit parallel to the edge of the peat bank, about 1 ft. (30 cm.) back, making a long slice that can be cut cross-ways into segments of turf for easy removal. This cut can also be made with the vertical wing of a peat spade, held back to front, or with the blade of a 'moor-spade' held sideways.

The handle-less Shetland 'moor-spade' closely resembles the small

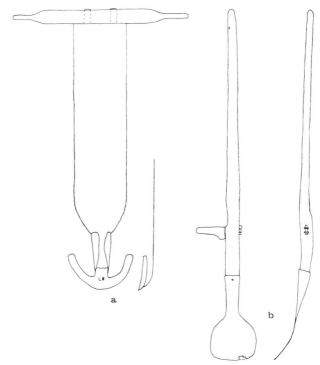

Fig. 22. (a) Flauchter spade, Shetland: Shetland County Museum; (b) moor spade, Orkney. In NMAS.

Shetland cultivating ('delving') spade in shape and dimensions, but lacks a foot-peg and has a more rounded blade (Fig. 21c, d), the purpose of which was to undercut and remove the turf previously sliced round the edges by the 'ripper', or by itself held sideways. It is paralleled in some respects by the larger and sturdier Orkney 'moor-spade'.

A third Shetland implement for cutting turf, not known elsewhere in Scotland, is found only in the south Mainland of Shetland and in Fair Isle (Fig. 22a). It has a cross-bar handle, a very broad, flat, straight shaft made from a plank, and a thin, crescent-shaped blade with a short, sharp upward curve at the head. At least one of the known examples was made by Laurence Brown, blacksmith in Lerwick. The specific purpose of this type was for cutting sods for thatching roofs, shaped so that they were thicker in the middle than at the sides, and could be smoothly overlapped on the roof like the scales of a fish. The very local character of this implement suggests that it was developed by

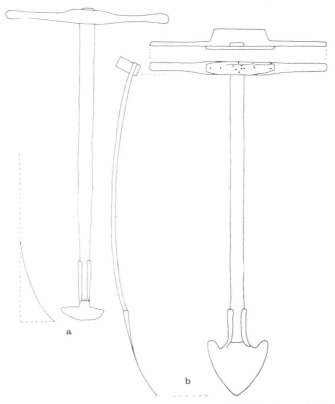

Fig. 23. Flauchter spades with straight shafts. (a) NMAS; (b) Angus Folk Collection, Glamis, Angus.

an ingenious individual in the area. The date of its origin has not been ascertained, but may not be much further back than the early 1900s.

Orkney

The strong Orkney moor spade (Fig. 22b) reflects an altogether different quality of turf. It has a stout shaft, thickened and slightly curved at its lower end, the broad spatulate blade continuing the curve evenly, so that the implement can act as a powerful lever. There is a foot-peg mortised through the thickest part of the shaft, and the shaft may have a short T-handle, or none at all.

In existing examples, the mouth of the blade is cut straight across, with the corners rounded from use. An illustration of c. 1770, however, which appears to show a similar type of tool, with a foot-peg, and curved back, has a pointed oval blade (Fenton 96 (1962-3), 308-9). To

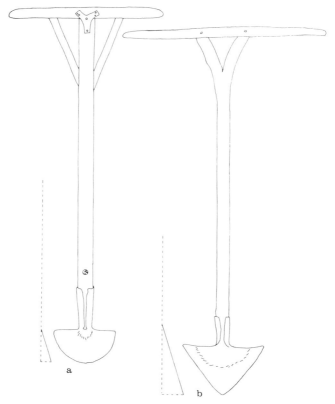

Fig. 24. (a) Flauchter spade, strutted shaft: Angus Folk Collection, Glamis, Angus; (b) flauchter spade, forked shaft: Stirling Museum.

this extent it is closer to the pointed form of the Scottish-mainland flauchter spade, whereas the straight mouth is more reminiscent of the local cultivating spade and peat spade.

Mainland Scotland

The flauchter spades of mainland Scotland are, within certain limits, fairly uniform in type. They all have cross-bar handles, and a shaft that may be straight or forked, or straight with a pair of struts (Fig. 24a). They may be joiner-made with neatly chamfered edges, like one from Glenesk, Angus, made by the Davidson family of joiners (Fig. 24b), or may be from a naturally forked piece of timber. One is made from the stave of a whisky cask (Fig. 23b). There is a majority of straight shafts amongst the examples examined, though this probably does no more than reflect the greater ease of obtaining timber for this form. There is no apparent regional significance in the distribution of straight and forked shafts; both may occur in the same area, and the straight shaft can be forked by the addition of struts. Commercial firms like Rigg & Sons, Sanquhar, Dumfriesshire, produced only straight-shafted flaughter spades, whereas the forked ones, which would have been more expensive to make commercially, are home- or joiner-made. Local joiners' account books contain a good deal of information on the range of shafts made. An East Lothian account book kept by the Foord family near Dunbar, has the following entries (Foord 1806-15):

6 August 1808.	To two shovel shafts for hedge spaids	...	...	...	1/6
	To a flaughter spaid shaft	...	...	...	1/6
	To a paidle [mattock-type hoe] shaft	...	...	...	6
1 April 1809	To 12 paidle shafts and put in do. at 6d		...	...	6/–
17 July 1812	To a pairing spaid handle	...	...	...	1/6

A slightly later account book in private possession, kept by the McKellar family at High Fenwick, Ayrshire, has the following:

I. 25 Nov. 1830	To a Flaughter sped heft ...	...	...	...	...	0.0.6
23 May 1833	To a pet barrow whell	...	...	...	...	0.2.6
II. 21 May 1834	To a pet sped shaft	...	...	...	...	0.1.6
23 May 1834	To a pet sped shaft	...	...	...	...	0.1.6

The blades range through a variety of shapes, rounded, heart-shaped, triangular, pointed half-oval, and crescentic (Figs. 23-25). The horned crescent of the Inverness example is rare (Fig. 25c). One shape may be moved into another through wear, or by being re-laid in the smithy, as in Fig. 24b where a rounded blade has become triangular. Many blades have been subjected to so much wear that only a small crescent of metal remains. In every case, the blades curve outwards regularly from the middle to the sides, and are dished to give a scooping action.

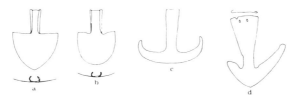

Fig. 25. Flaughter spade blades, (a) Angus, 1890: Stirling Museum; (b) Dunblane, Perthshire: Stirling Museum; (c) Leanach Cottage, Culloden, Inverness; (d) Galloway. All in NMAS.

In Dumfries and Galloway, in the south-west of Scotland, a blade of local form (Fig. 25d) is found. It has an arrow-shaped head, with one wing of the arrow considerably extended, so that, when turned on its side, the wing can serve as a 'ripper'. It is so close in form to the Galloway peat spade, discussed below, that it could be converted to a peat spade simply by bending the long wing forward at right angles.

Flaughter spades vary in length from about 3½ to 6 ft. (107 to 183 cm.) long, with the majority about 4½ to 5 ft. (137 to 152 cm.). Since, in cutting turf, the blade has to run parallel with the ground, the length of the shaft has an effect on the angle of the blade. It can be seen that a shorter shaft demands a sharper blade angle, and that the blade angle may also be affected by the curvature of the shaft.

Very occasionally, flaughter spades have a vertical wing at one side of the blade, like peat spades and the English breast spade. Only two examples have been noted, one in the Nairn Museum, the other in the Museum of Ironmongery in Selkirk and said to be from the Ettrick area. In both cases the blade is broad, pointed, and quite flat, the wing extending along the full length of one side. The cross-bar handle of the Ettrick flaughter spade is strengthened by two metal struts. These may reflect the influence of the breast spade, but their shafts are much shorter — the Ettrick spade is only 3 ft. 4 in. (99 cm.) long overall — and this type may be seen as an amalgam of the breast and flaughter spades, with the blade and wing of one and the shaft length of the other.

Peat Spades

It is not intended here to examine the background and techniques of peat cutting, but merely to look at the typological range of peat spades, since these frequently form part of a work group with turf spades, and on occasion the formal influence of one may be seen on the other. Eight main geographical groups emerge, each of which, though overlapping with its neighbours, has spades with clear regional characteristics. The following notes form a preliminary study that will require amplification in the future.

Shetland

In Shetland the standard peat spade is a slim tool with a straight shaft of which the lower part is flat, and, with the blade, slightly concave in

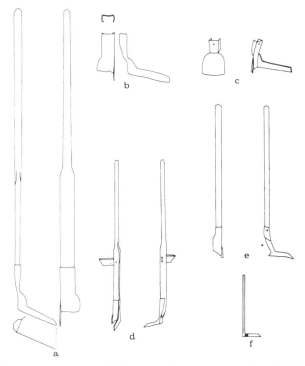

Fig. 26. Shetland tuskers, a-b, 1:10, remainder, not to scale; (a) Shetland County Museum; (b) NMAS; (c) delving spade and tusker blades, made by T. Black & Sons, Berwick-on-Tweed, after Catalogue; (d) Shetland tusker, after Svabo (1781-2) 1959; (e) after Shirreff 1814; (f) after Hibbert 1822. The shaded portion indicates the flange.

front (Fig. 26b) to create a certain amount of suction to hold the cut peat in place. There is a relatively long wing, up to 7 in. (18 cm.) long. At the opposite side of the blade from the wing there is a forward-curved feather (Fig. 26a).

The blades are made in four stages. First a blank of mild steel is cut out. It is about 1 ft. (30 cm.) long by 2 in. (5 cm.) wide, with an offset tang at one end. The blank is heated, and the tang bent nearly, but not quite, at right angles, and drawn out to form the wing. Next the body is beaten out, leaving a constricted neck at the junction of the blade and the socket. At this stage the piece is completely flat and the wing lies in the same plane as the blade and socket. Finally the socket flanges are turned back, the wing brought forward at right angles to the blade, and the feather at the opposite side turned up in a rounded curve away from the plane of the blade. Most Shetland blades were made by local smiths, but could also be bought from commercial firms like Black of

Berwick-on-Tweed in the north of England, who made irons for both peat and cultivating spades (Fig. 26c).

The earliest illustration (Fig. 26d) of a Shetland peat spade dates from c. 1782 in a book about the Faroe Islands. Faroese peat spades have no wings, and the author commented that in Shetland a man could cut twice as much peat in the same length of time, for only one cutting movement was necessary instead of two (Djurhuus 1959, 136, 139). The next illustration dates from 1814 (Shirreff 1814, facing 51) (Fig. 26e). The chief difference between it and surviving examples is that the shaft is round all the way down to the blade. The wing has the same downwards rake, but the blade, instead of being cut square across at the mouth, is angled, and there is an angular feather, which does not appear to curve forward, at the side opposite the wing. On the other hand, however, the earlier illustration of 1782 (Fig. 26d) from the Faroe Islands shows a peat spade much closer in form to the present-day Shetland spade, with the lower part of the shaft flattened to carry long, narrow peats when they are being lifted, and a forward-curved feather opposite the wing. It differs only in having a foot-peg at one side. A Shetland illustration of 1822, however, again appears to show a shaft rounded all the way down to the blade, though since it is drawn from the side only this cannot be quite certain (Fig. 26f). The shaft was said to be rather longer than that of the common (Shetland) spade, with 'a feather [wing] projecting in one place 7 ins. [18 cm.], in another little more than an inch [2.5 cm.]' (Hibbert 1822, 430 and Plate VI, Fig. 23). This smaller projection may refer to the feather.

Whatever variations in form existed in the late eighteenth and early nineteenth centuries, only one type occurs at the present day.

A characteristic of the Shetland peat spade is that it has no foot-peg, and is operated by the arms alone. The operator thrusts it down the face of the bank, from the top, at a slight angle, and cuts a peat measuring about 14 in. long by 7 in. broad by 2½ in. thick (35.5 x 16 x 6 cm.) (Edmonston I (1809), 176). He then lifts the cut peat and throws it with the spade to the place at the top or bottom of the bank, where it will get its first few days of drying. He has no assistant in this work, unlike peat workers in most other parts of Scotland.

The only part of Shetland so far noted where a different tool is used is Fair Isle, where the hard, brittle quality of the peat has led to its being dug with the common Shetland cultivating spade (Fig. 26c).

The Shetland peat spade is called a 'tusker', from Norse *torfskeri*, implying a Norse ancestry.

Orkney and Caithness

Both Orkney and Caithness have peat spades, also called 'tuskers', that are similar to the Shetland 'tusker', but of sturdier construction, reflecting the tougher quality of Orkney peat. According to a Caithness description of 1812:

> They have two modes of cutting peats, horizontal, and perpendicular; *i.e.* when the peat moss is not more than from one to two feet [30.4-60.9 cm.] deep, the peat is cut perpendicularly, by a spade, called a *turskill* [sic]. This instrument is about nine inches [22.9 cm.] long, with a heel at right angles to the right side, two inches and a half [6.3 cm.] broad, with a perpendicular socket, (being the continuance of the heel), to embrace the wooden handle, about four feet and a half [137 cm.] long; and in it is fixed a *foot-step* of wood, a few inches above the termination of the socket of the spade. The peat-cutter, holding the handle with both hands, with one push of the right foot, drives the spade into the moss, so as to cut a peat, or turf, 12 inches [30.4 cm.] long, and two inches [5 cm.] thick: the breadth of the heel regulates the thickness of the peat. A woman stands at the bottom of the bank, whose business it is to seize the peat, as soon as the cutter gives it a jerk, to separate it from the bottom, and she throws it on the right side of the bank, where people are employed to spread them to dry. The mode of cutting peat horizontally, is the mode practised in many districts, and is too well known to require being particularly described (Henderson 1812, 234).

One Orkney example that is particularly close in appearance to those from Shetland is initialled 'LB' on the back of the blade (Fig. 27a), and it is quite possible that it was made in Lerwick by the well-known blacksmith, Laurence Brown. This one is hand-operated, but the majority of the Orkney and Caithness 'tuskers' have foot-pegs (Fig. 27b), and also differ in the considerable size of the wing, which may be up to 12 in. (30.5 cm.) long. It follows that Orkney peats are broader than Shetland peats, since the breadth of the peat is here decided by the length of the wing. There was the further difference that in these areas, when the man was cutting the peat, he had an assistant or '*oot-taker*', usually a woman, to take the peats as they were cut, and fling them up to dry (Firth (1920), 107-8). The size and weight of these 'tuskers' would have made it an excessive labour for the operator to throw up the peat himself.

The good-quality, black peats cut with the 'tusker' were called 'tusker peats', and when, in the nineteenth century, there was an active trade in peat fuel between Orkney and the Firth of Forth, these were kept for sale, and the inferior sandy or moor peat was used for home consumption. The name 'tusker' was also adopted as a unit of

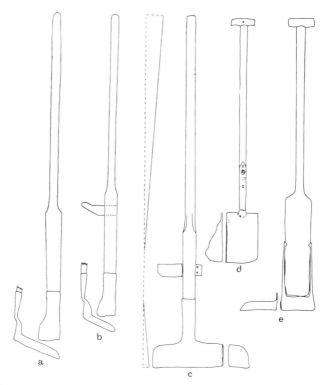

Fig. 27. (a) Tusker, no foot-peg, Orkney, perhaps made in Shetland: NMAS; (b) tusker, Orkney: NMAS; (c) luggie, Orkney: NMAS; (d) iron-bladed spade, Orkney: NMAS; (e) shield, for tough hill peat, Caithness: NMAS.

measurement in peat cutting, applied to the amount of peat a 'tuskerman' could cut in a day of about twelve hours, from sunrise to sunset. This commercial activity cleared extensive tracts of land, for example in the area of Stenness, where full-scale agriculture is now carried on (Leask I.iv (1907), 129, 133-4).

For the inferior, shallow, hill peat a special implement, not known outside Orkney, was developed. The shaft is like that of a 'tusker', with a stout foot-peg, and the blade is very broad, like a rectangle placed broadways on the end of the shaft, with a vertical wing on one side (Fig. 27c). Presumably because the blade projects like an ear at each side of the shaft, it is locally called a 'luggie' (Marwick 1929 s.v.) (the 'eared spade'). In this case the mouth of the blade is broad and the wing short, reversing the state of affairs with the 'tusker' where the mouth is short and the wing long.

The term 'luggie' is Scots in origin, but of the score and more of technical terms in Orkney connected with peat cutting and different qualities of peat a high proportion is Norse. Whatever the truth of the story that the tenth-century Torf-Einar got his nickname from being the first to cut peat for fuel, because of the scarcity of timber (Taylor 1938, 141; Pálsson and Edwards 1978, 32), there is no doubt that peat cutting was a practice in which the Viking settlers indulged extensively.

Commercially made peat spades with solid iron blades of rectangular form, like a garden spade, with a short wing at one side (Fig. 27d), are also used in Orkney.

Besides the 'tusker', Caithness also has a particular type of peat spade known as a 'shield' (Fig. 27e). The word, with intrusive *d*, is the same as 'shiel', a dialect word meaning 'to shovel', and in Caithness the term 'sheeled peat' is applied to peat cut horizontally, with a shovelling action. The 'shield' has a long, rectangular blade of wood shod with iron and a wing 4 to 5 in. (10 to 13 cm.) long with no upwards or downwards rake. This was the spade used in Caithness for shallow hill peat. Unlike the Orkney 'luggie', however, it was worked with the arms alone. For this reason its rate of production was not as high as that of the foot-operated 'tusker'. The 'shield' required two women to help with lifting and spreading the peat, whereas the 'tusker' could keep three spreaders employed.

Highlands and Islands

In this large area, a certain amount of variation and overlap is inevitable, especially in the southern parts, in the Inner Hebrides, Argyll, and so on, but in the north and north-west the striking point is the broad similarity of the spades in use. Generally speaking they have no handle on the end of the shafts, though handles of horn or wood appear in Glencoe, Arran, western Perthshire (Fig. 28g, h), and elsewhere, just as in south-west Scotland and parts of Ireland. They are asymmetrical, since the shaft is set at one side to allow for a wooden tread (Gaelic: *smeachan*), the lower end of which runs into the socket of the blade alongside the shaft, so that the shaft and tread together fill the width of the socket and form an extension to the length of the blade. Alternatively the tread and shaft may be cut out of one piece. A foot-peg mortised into the shaft, in the manner of the Orkney and Caithness 'tusker', is comparatively rare. One example of this has been noted, now preserved by the National Trust for Scotland in Leanach Cottage, Culloden, Inverness (Fig. 28c).

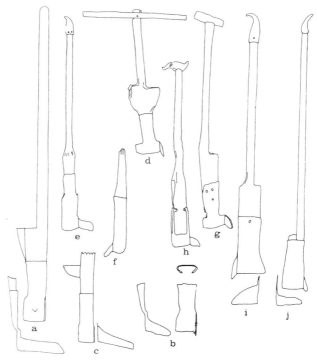

Fig. 28. Peat spades, (a) Tarbat, Easter Ross: NMAS; (b) Skye: NMAS; (c) Glencoe Museum; (d) no scale, Dunphail, Moray: Highland Folk Museum; (e) no scale, Mull: Highland Folk Museum; (f) no scale, Mull: Highland Folk Museum; (g) no scale, Laggan, Inverness-shire: Highland Folk Museum; (h) no scale, probably west Highlands: Stirling Museum; (i, j) probably west Highlands: Stirling Museum.

The long wings have the characteristic downward rake of the wings on 'tusker' blades in Orkney and Shetland, which means that they lie horizontally when the shaft is tilted back at the proper cutting angle. At the side of the blade opposite the wing (Gaelic: *sgiath*), there is often, but not by any means always, a flat feather (Fig. 28a, b), with no forward curve. It may be significant that the same feature is present in the 1814 illustration of a Shetland peat spade (Fig. 26c), pointing to an earlier feature that has disappeared in that area, but survived elsewhere.

The Gaelic name for this kind of peat spade is *toirisgeir* or *toirsgian*, the former cognate with 'tusker', the latter showing the assimilation of the Gaelic word for knife (*sgian*) to the second element of the original form, producing a hybrid term.

In the southerly parts of the Inner Hebrides and the eastern

Highlands a variety of peat-spade forms occurs, but otherwise the 'tusker' form prevails, marked by a comparatively narrow iron blade with a relatively long wing that has an invariable downward rake, a shaft with no handle or backward-turned horn, a foot-peg projecting from the side of the shaft or a tread attached to or forming part of the shaft, which is always placed asymmetrically, and, frequently, with a flat or curved feather at the opposite side of the blade from the wing. Its exact distribution in the Highlands has not yet been fully ascertained, though from the evidence of museum specimens, illustrations in documentary sources, and personal observation, the pattern appears to form a crescent covering the Northern Isles, Caithness, the north-west Highlands and Outer Hebrides, and south at least to Skye. The distribution coincides in part with the areas of Scandinavian settlement, and is continued southwards by the type of peat spade known in Ireland as the 'slane' (Evans 1957, 190-1). The 'tusker', therefore, appears to point back to a period of cultural unity in this crescentic area. However, the same crescent can be traced in other ways, for example by the forms of certain types of draught yoke found in peat bogs, and since these may be pre-Norse, it would be unwise to over-stress an ethnic argument with regard to 'tuskers', though their Norse name is, of course, significant. Within this broad group, one of the major variations is due to the fact that in Shetland, alone in Scotland, the peat cutter regularly lays out the peat for drying without an assistant, so that his implement has to become lighter, and the top of the blade and lower part of the shaft concave to produce enough suction to hold the peat in position during lifting. This was no problem when an assistant stood by to remove the cut peat, in which case the concavity was unnecessary. Whatever the ultimate explanation, it can be said that here the socio-ergonomic background has considerably affected the appearance of the peat spade, though without altering its basic character.

A miscellaneous group of peat spades is also found in the Highlands and Hebrides, particularly in the eastern and southern districts, some of which derive from the 'tusker', and some from the types of the adjacent Lowlands. Some of these are very crude, such as an example from Dunphail, Moray, with a crossbar handle like a flauchter spade (Fig. 28d). Its blade, however, certainly came originally from a shaft of better quality, and is matched by the blade of a spade from Laggan, Inverness; both blades are broadways rectangular, winged for their full depth, and in these respects like the Orkney 'luggie'. Both spades have

E

cross-bar handles, and were undoubtedly used for cutting tough hill peat.

Two spades from Mull (Fig. 28e, f) and one from Arran (Fig. 28h) are symmetrical, without foot-pegs or treads. One has a horn handle, one a curved wooden handle, and the top of the third is broken. These must come from areas of good-quality, soft peat. The blades are broader than 'tusker' blades, and the wings shorter, without the downward rake. Two have all-metal blades, one has an iron-shod wooden blade, but in all cases part of the shaft is flattened to give additional support to the peat.

Two horn-handled spades in Stirling Museum have iron blades that flare out to the mouth to give a broader cut, and treads for the feet. The wings are perpendicular, with no downward rake (Fig. 28i, j). Though unprovenanced, they probably come from the west mainland of Scotland. A treaded spade from Laggan, Inverness-shire has a broadways rectangular blade (Fig. 28g).

In the Highlands and Hebrides, much recording and documentation remains to be done, and the significance and distributional patterns of some of these variations will no doubt become clearer in the future. It may be suggested, however, that because of their miscellaneous nature, some of these spades are likely to be later in the dates of their introduction than the 'tusker' itself.

North-East Scotland

In the areas so far discussed, all the peat spades have had straight-mouthed, narrow blades with long wings. In north-east Scotland, however, from as far north as Morayshire and south into Angus and the Mearns, the great majority have round-mouthed, broad blades with relatively short wings. They average just over 3 ft. (91 cm.) long in contrast to the just over 4 ft. (122 cm.) length of their northerly and westerly fellows.

In the flat bog lands of the Buchan district of Aberdeenshire, and also in the higher-lying bogs of Aberdeenshire and Banffshire, two types of peat spades were (and are) in use, the 'breist spade' (breasting spade) and the 'stamp spade' (underfoot spade). The latter was worked vertically, and was so-called because it was stamped down with the foot. The breasting spade was worked horizontally into the peat from the face or breast of the bank, the operator standing at the bottom. Most of the homes in the district have both types, either being used according to the wetness of the bog or season, but the breasting spade

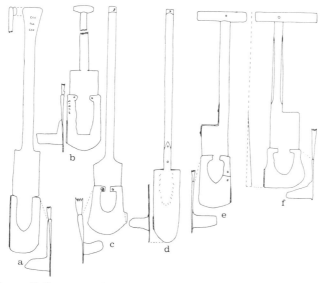

Fig. 29. (a, b, c, d) Breast spades, north-east Scotland: NMAS; (e, f) stamp spades, north-east Scotland: NMAS.

is commonest. Besides the amount of moisture, the nature of the peat deposit itself is a strong conditioning factor in the type of tool used. This was clearly demonstrated by Mr Will. Strachan who works annually in the Crombie Moss, near Marnoch, Banffshire, a high-lying bog filling the basin of what must have been a lake in times past, where the amber seeds of bog-bean are found overlying the clay 20 ft. (6.1 m.) or so down in the peat. The peat layers are deposited here in narrow, horizontal strata, so that if cut from the top, the strata would lie across the peat, which on drying would break into numerous small rectangles. If cut in from the face with the breasting spade, however, the strata lie longitudinally, and the peat does not break up during drying. Naturally enough, the breast spade is the only one used in the bog.

The breasting spade is a perfectly symmetrical tool, usually with a T-handle and an iron-shod wooden blade, quite flat in front, and slightly rounded at the back. One spade, an early example but not definitely dated, has a finger-grip instead of a T-handle and the blade is longer and narrower than most of the more recent examples (Fig. 29a). All blades have rounded mouths, some being semi-circular (Fig. 29b, c). Some blades are straight-sided, others flare out towards the mouth in a somewhat bell-shaped fashion (Fig. 29c). The wings are vertical, or have an upward rake. The form is also reproduced in all-metal blades (Fig. 29d).

The underfoot spade is a functionally developed type that, more than any other tool, characterises the bogs of Buchan. It has a shaft set asymmetrically at one side to leave a solid tread, usually metal-plated, at the top of the wooden blade. The cross-bar handle is also set asymmetrically so that the longer side overlies the tread. In this way, when working in a deep bog and cutting a second or third depth of peat, it is possible to get close in to the inner face of the bank without grazing the spade and hand against it. It is remarkable for its extreme shortness, only a little over 2½ ft. (76 cm.). The mouth is again rounded, with a tendency for the sides to flare out (Fig. 29e, f).

In Buchan, quantities of peat are still cut annually, and besides the crofters and farmers who secure their winter's supply of fuel, there were professional peat workers like James Strachan in the New Pitsligo area, who combined this job with the craft of thatching, for which the cutting of sods to underlie the thatch was a normal preliminary. Such people kept a range of well-cared-for tools. Mr Strachan had a set of seven: a 'bullin' spade', a 'turned bullin' spade', a 'stumper' or 'stamp spade', two 'breisters' or 'breist spades', two 'tirrin' spades'. The 'tirrin' spades' were used like flaughter spades in removing the turf layer above the peat bank. Next, the 'bullin' spade' was used to undercut the peat so that the peat spade itself had only to cut the sides of the slab of peat, the bottom being already sheared. The ordinary 'bullin' spade' was used for undercutting the first and second depths of peat. For the third and usually the lowermost depth, the 'turned bullin' spade' came into its own. Whereas the first was quite straight, with an absolutely flat blade and shaft in the same plane, the 'turned bullin' spade' was a tool with lift. It could therefore be pushed horizontally into the bottom of the bank without getting the handle into the mire, and it also saved bending. Mr Strachan's kit was completed by two breasting spades and one underfoot spade, all flaring towards the mouth.

Angus and the Mearns

This area can be differentiated from north-east Scotland on two main counts. On the one hand, it has no asymmetrical underfoot spades; on the other, the majority of spades examined, though similar to the symmetrical breasting spades in the north-east, are intended to be pressed in with the foot, and the treads at one or both sides of the shaft at the top of the blade are often lined with leather to minimise wear or to

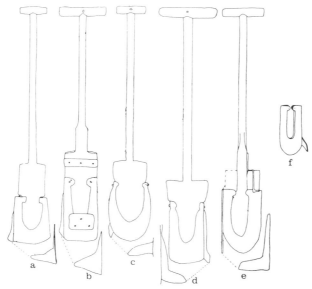

Fig. 30. (a, b, e) Peat spades, Glenesk, Angus; (c) Glen Prosen, Angus: Stirling Museum; (d) Angus Folk Collection, Glamis, Angus; (f) no scale, round-mouthed peat-spade iron, made by T. Black & Sons, Berwick-on-Tweed, after Catalogue.

bring a worn tread back to the level. They also differ from the breasting spades of the north-east in having, as a rule, cross-bar handles up to 1 ft. (30.5 cm.) long. Breasting spades with T-handles also occur, though they appear to be in the minority (Fig. 30a).

Another noticeable characteristic is that the wing is often continued in a narrow extension that runs most of the way along the side of the iron shoe, or in the case of all-iron blades, all the way up the side of the blade. The wings conform to those of the north-east in being vertical or raked upwards, and some are curved slightly upwards (Fig. 30a, b, e), a feature that normally goes with breasting spades, though as previously noted, these often have treads and can also be used underfoot.

Iron-bladed spades (Fig. 31a, b, c, d) are more numerous than in the north-east, and many of those examined were stamped 'T. Black, Ford Forge' on the blades, as were the blades of turf and draining spades. This firm was situated in Northumberland and its products were popular as far north as Angus, though no examples have been noted farther north. Most of the iron blades are rectangular, with originally straight mouths slightly rounded from use. The older iron-shod blades were made rounded in the mouth, and their tendency to flare is only

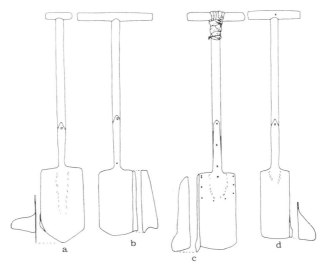

Fig. 31. (a) Peat spade: Angus Folk Collection, Glamis, Angus; (b, c, d) peat spades, Glenesk, Angus.

exceptionally reproduced in the iron blades; the one example noted, made by T. Black, has in addition a pointed mouth, and resembles a spade made by the firm of T. Black & Sons, Berwick-on-Tweed (Fig. 31b), apparently a related firm. T. Black & Sons also produced round-mouthed iron shoes for wooden peat spades, presumably for sale in the north-east and Angus where these were popular. Spades with rounded mouths could have straight or convex sides (Fig. 30c, d, e).

Wherever information was available about spades with all-iron blades, it appeared that they were mainly of twentieth-century date. As a rule their present owners had not bought them direct from a firm, but had acquired them at farm sales, so that their first home and date could not be pinpointed readily. In general, however, most reached Angus during the period about 1910-20.

Central Scotland

To the south-west, in Perthshire and Stirlingshire, the round-mouthed blades tail off in numbers. Instead there are square-mouthed wooden blades with iron shoes (Fig. 32a, b, c, d), or square-mouthed rectangular iron blades like those in Angus. One round-mouthed, iron shoe from the area comes, as might be expected, from Alyth in east Perthshire, just across the border from Angus.

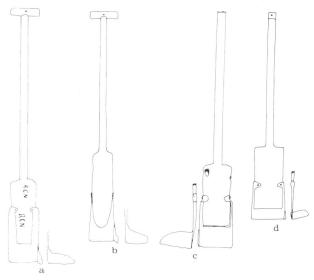

Fig. 32. Peat spades, central Scotland, (a, b) Stirling Museum; (c) NMAS; (d) Ardvorlich, Lochearnhead, Perthshire: NMAS.

The wings are usually vertical, though one example (Fig. 32d) has an upward-raked wing welded on to the shoe.

All the examples noted are breasting spades, and the nearest Scottish equivalents appear to be the Caithness 'shield' (which is, however, a much bigger implement) and perhaps the spades of south-east Scotland (Fig. 34). The type is also known in east-central Europe, and one example is preserved in the museum at Templin, Brandenburg. It is said to have been characteristic of that area (Schmidt 3 (1957), 394 and Plate XVa).

South-West Scotland

The spades of south-west Scotland, particularly Galloway and Dumfries, have a number of distinct regional features. They have an average length of 3½ to 4 ft. (107-122 cm.), and the wooden shaft has either a horn handle, as in Argyll, the Inner Hebrides and Ireland, or a back-turned piece of hard wood scarfed on to the end. Very rarely, there is a small T-handle (Fig. 33a, b).

The lower third of the shaft broadens out to provide a flat surface, but the socket of the iron blade is gradually drawn in to form a narrow neck instead of maintaining the lower-shaft width all the way down. The blade then swells out in the form of a heart, of which one lobe is

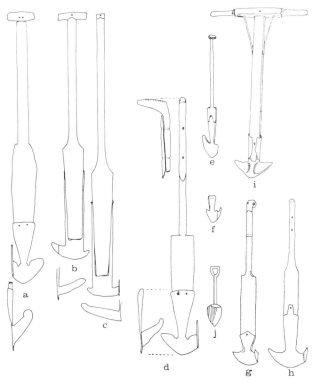

Fig. 33. Peat spades, south-west Scotland, (a, b, c, d) NMAS; (e) no scale, 'Galloway Pattern', made by J. Rigg & Sons, Sanquhar, Dumfriesshire, after Catalogue; (f) no scale, 'Ordinary Pattern' peat-spade blade, made by J. Rigg & Sons, after Catalogue; (g) no scale, ordinary peat spade, made by T. Thomson, blacksmith, Lochhead of Elrig, Wigtownshire; (h) no scale, peat spade for hill peat, made by T. Thomson, blacksmith; (i) no scale, flauchter spade, made by T. Thomson, blacksmith; (j) no scale, spade used in fens, Lincolnshire, after Mortimer, 1708.

turned at right angles to provide a wing raked steeply upwards, the other lobe remaining as a feather (Fig. 33a, d). The type has been perpetuated and disseminated through its manufacture by local spade-making firms like James Rigg & Sons at Sanquhar, established in 1772, and William Cotts at Penpont, established in 1843. The former firm illustrates in its catalogue a peat spade described as 'Galloway Pattern', with a blade lobed at one side only, and lacking a vertical wing. In their catalogue illustration, the short T-handle is set at right angles to the plane of the blade, possibly a cheaper adaptation of the back-turned handle of wood or horn (Fig. 33e). No existing examples of this type have so far been noted, and the spade normally used is the one described by Rigg as 'Ordinary Pattern', with a feather and wing as described above (Fig. 33f). A source of 1812 speaks of a small iron works in Kirkconnel, above Sanquhar, employing eight men and making three to four dozen spades a day (Singer 1812, 421).

Two examples of another type have been noted (Fig. 33b, c). Instead of sockets with constricted necks, and heart-shaped blades, these have crescentic iron shoes with long straps nailed to the sides of the wooden blade. The wings are raked slightly upwards. This blade form approximates to that of the flauchter spade, and the reason may be that it was used for cutting tougher hill peat.

Mr T. Thomson, the late blacksmith at Lochhead of Elrig in Wigtownshire, a maker of highly regarded spades, produced not only peat spades with heart-shaped blades, but also a much wider, crescentic type, 9½ in. (24 cm.) across for cutting shallow, single-depth hill peats. As can be seen (Fig. 33g, h), the blade is remarkably similar to that of the flauchter spade, which worked in equivalent conditions, though there is, of course, no lift in the peat spade.

The heart-shaped blade also occurs on flauchter spades (Fig. 23b) and is paralleled on a type of spade (Fig. 33j) used in the Lincolnshire fens about the year 1700, with a blade,

> . . . the Edges of which are as sharp as a Knife, which makes it easy to cut Flag-roots, and the Roots of other Weeds, and indeed is very useful in any Lands that have not stones in them; some of the Spades are made with one side turned up like a Breast Plough, by which means they with once jobbing of it into the Ground, can cut an exact Turf, so that one Man with one of these Spades in fenny soft Ground, will do as much as two Men with a common Spade (Mortimer 1708, 286-7).

This duality seems to provide a parallel type of development on the analogy of which it may be suggested that the Galloway peat spade, whether in its crescentic or heart-shaped form, owes a good deal to the flauchter spade, and to the nature of the peat in which it was used.

The Galloway spade was used for breasting, except in very wet weather or in very wet areas, when the work was done underfoot by cutting vertically at a slight angle from the top of the bank.

South-East Scotland

The surviving evidence from this area is scanty, and is confined at the moment to four iron blades in the Wilton Lodge Museum, Hawick. One blade is from a Galloway spade. Two are square-mouthed iron shoes, with lateral straps for attachment to the wooden blade, similar to the spades from central Scotland (Fig. 34a).

Fig. 34. Peat spade irons, south-east Scotland, (a, b) Wilton Lodge Museum, Hawick; (c) 'Irish Pattern', made by T. Black & Sons, Berwick-on-Tweed, after Catalogue. No scales.

The fourth example (Fig. 34b) has a broadways-rectangular blade on the end of the socket, with two flat feathers from the outer side of one of which the wing extends. The whole blade is twice as wide as it is deep. It resembles a type made by Black & Sons in Berwick-on-Tweed (Fig. 34c), described as 'Irish Pattern' in their catalogue.

It is something of a coincidence that in this same area there is a find of what may be a Romano-British peat spade of about the second century A.D., in a hoard of metalwork from Blackburn Mill (Fenton 96 (1962-63), 271-2), also with a feather on each side from one of which the wing rises (Fig. 35). The ratio of width to depth is different, about 1:1, but otherwise the similarity is remarkable. Since the Blackburn Mill blade is probably the earliest known peat spade that can be identified as such and approximately dated, the flat feather opposite the wing can be regarded as an early feature, and as has been shown earlier, it also occurs on the blades of 'tuskers' in the north and west that may go back to Viking times.

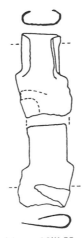

Fig. 35. Winged peat spade blade, Blackburn Mill Hoard, Berwickshire. In NMAS.

Commercial Spade-Making Firms

This survey of peat and turf spades in museum collections and on farms and crofts in Scotland shows that in spite of the dissemination of commercially produced articles, regional varieties are still in use. Indeed, the spade-making firms themselves acknowledged the strength of local demand by including local types in their range of goods. T. Black & Sons, Berwick-on-Tweed, established in 1788, made Shetland cultivating-spade blades and 'tuskers' (Fig. 26c), as well as round-mouthed iron shoes for the peat spades of north-east Scotland and Angus, and the feathered 'Irish Pattern' peat spade (*Black*, n.d.). The Holm Forge Company, Glasgow, which concentrated on industrial spades and shovels, made 'solid steel Dumfries spades' with pointed mouths (*Holm*, n.d.), as also did George Wolfe & Sons of Bathgate, established in 1877. The latter firm also bowed to national preference by supplying garden spades with either the 'Scotch crutch' (a straight-topped T-handle) or the 'English crutch' (a T-handle of which the ends curved slightly down) (*Wolfe*, n.d.). James Rigg & Sons, Sanquhar, Dumfries, established in 1772 and calling itself 'the oldest firm in the trade in Scotland', made so-called 'Derry and Newry' spades (similar to the 'Dumfries' spades of two firms but unlike spades used in the Derry and Newry areas in northern Ireland) and Yorkshire spades (*Rigg*, n.d.). Even wholesale ironmongers in Edinburgh were catering for markets as far away as Shetland by supplying blades for Shetland spades and 'tuskers' (perhaps supplied to them by Black of Berwick-on-Tweed) (*Scott*, n.d.).

From the third quarter of the eighteenth century, therefore, Scottish firms were disseminating their wares. English tools were being introduced before this, for improving landlords like Grant of Monymusk in Aberdeenshire were getting steel-bladed shovels via Leith already in 1735 (Hamilton 1946, 25). English influence was also responsible for the establishment of some forges, such as the Cadell Iron Works at Cramond, on the outskirts of Edinburgh. Here,

> . . . the spade and shovel branch was introduced . . . by one Richard Squires from Newcastle, a worthy, capital, and industrious workman, greatly superior to any in that line in Scotland. The works of his own hand are easily distinguished; and are in particular request even in London. About 1000 dozen of spades and shovels, . . . are annually manufactured at these works.

In the summer of 1792, the firm had eight spademakers at work (Wood 1794, 91, 112; Skinner 1965, 27-9).

Though commercialisation from the last decades of the eighteenth century did not kill the regional varieties, neither did it foster their survival, for it is commercially uneconomic to produce a large number of slightly varying types. In spite of the output of the Scottish firms for regional purposes, it must be remembered that they were for the most part situated in or near the industrial areas, and their main range of products was calculated to meet industrial demand for implements used in activities like mining, shovelling coke and railway work, whether they were using water-driven tilt hammers of the type that remained until recently at the Barblues Forge, Airdrie or more up-to-date kinds of power as at the Chieftain Forge, Bathgate, where draining and forestry spades are still produced in fair numbers. Spades for agricultural purposes, including peat and turf cutting, formed a much smaller part of their output, and it was left to the general-purpose blacksmith to supply much of the local demand for spades of a specialist nature, in collaboration with the joiner and the home handyman. For this reason, commercial firms have not even yet much affected implements like turf and peat spades, and particularly peat spades of which at least eight regional groups are still definable. The main effect of the forges has been in partially replacing iron-shod wooden blades by all-iron blades, these having as a rule rectangular shapes, like garden spades, with strap sockets. What is really leading to the disappearance of the peat and turf spades is the disuse of peat as fuel in many areas, for in terms of time and transport costs, peat is often more expensive than coal.

6

Peat in Fetlar in the 1960s

The island of Fetlar is one of the North Isles of Shetland, lying east of the island of Yell, with Hascosay in the sound between. In size it measures roughly six miles by four, and though it is regarded as one of the most fertile areas in Shetland, the extent of arable has greatly receded since about the mid-nineteenth century. In the northerly parts and in Lamb Hoga peninsula in the south-west this was due to displacement of the population so that the area could be turned into pasture for sheep, and in the townships at the south side it is partly due to the inability of crofters, some of whom are getting on in years, to make full use of the arable potential. A manuscript list, dated 1826, of the communicant inhabitants of Fetlar gives over 800 names. I am indebted to Mr Thomason, Vailzie, and his sister Mrs M. Hughson, Leagarth, for allowing me to examine the list. The present (1964) total population is about 120, making a reduction in adult numbers of over 85% in the last 150 years.

The average size of the present crofts is about 20 acres, with an average cultivable area of about two acres. The units of land utilisation are fragmented in a form of fossilised runrig, so that in a township each man owns rigs or parts of rigs mixed up with those of his neighbours. This inevitably wastes a great deal of working time, and the situation is aggravated when a man inherits or is assigned another croft which may not even be in the same township.

This background has to be borne in mind when considering the question of cutting and transporting peat for fuel. In the days when the population was large, there would always have been enough folk to keep the work going both at home and at the peat bank. Although the population was formerly 85% larger, the former amount of arable is nothing like 85% greater, so that the available land must have been more intensively cultivated. According to Low in 1774, the arable produced 'Corn nearly sufficient for the inhabitants in ordinary years' (Low 1879, 164-5). At this time, they numbered 500-600.

Until the late 1950s, peat was the main fuel of the island. Some was cut at Everland on the east side, but was sulphury and unpleasant on

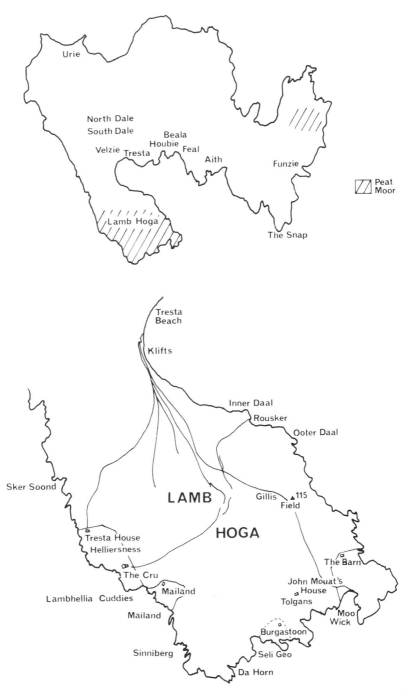

Fig. 36. Top: the island of Fetlar, showing the peat-bearing areas and the townships.

Below: the peninsula of Lamb Hoga, showing peat-tracks, areas of former settlement and surviving 'peat-houses'.

the fire, producing ashes of a terra-cotta colour. Apart from this, supplies were drawn almost entirely from Lamb Hoga, the only part of Fetlar that bears peat in any quantity. This peninsula is more or less remote from the townships (Fig. 36), and with a reduced population, the time and effort involved in casting and transporting peat played a real part in inhibiting attempts at improvement. The same lack of manpower finally led to the cessation of peat casting and flitting in the 1950s.

At the present time coal is brought in at a cost of £15 a ton and has to be ferried in a flit boat, in sacks, from the steamer. £1500 to £2000 goes out of the island annually for coal, even though driftwood helps out the domestic economy. It is unlikely that the saving in time can yet be said to counterbalance this expenditure, but it may do so eventually as schemes for the reclamation of hill land by drainage and re-seeding (subsequent to apportionment), and of the re-grouping of each crofter's rigs into unified blocks, are proceeded with.

Peat, therefore, played a real part in Fetlar's social and economic structure by its presence, and continues to play a concealed part by its absence. Work amongst the peat in this island is now a matter of history. Without exception, the inhabitants look back at the days on the peat-bank with nostalgia, hard though the work was, and regard it as having been the highlight of the yearly work-cycle, a unique social occasion based on collaborative effort. The notes that follow, based on fieldwork carried out in August 1963, aim at providing a factual record of an aspect of community life that has only just passed away, after a decline that has lasted for at least two centuries, for already in 1774 Low saw that many of the Fetlar folk got their peat from Yell, since they were 'not so happily situated in this particular' (*Ib.*).

Cutting and drying

Peat cutting began in May and was chiefly done by men. The first task was to rip the peat-bank and remove the surface turf. This process was known as *flaa-ing* (flaying) the bank, and could be done in two ways. The first involved the moor-spade (Fig. 37, left), and was the one in use until the comparatively recent introduction of *rippers*. Two spades were used, and the flaaers worked together. Quite often a woman handled the top spade, which was the common delving spade, and would cut the *feal* or turf across the surface to the breadth required, and a man would cut underneath with a moor spade. The blade of the

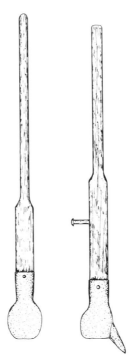

Fig. 37. A *moor-spade* (left), 4 ft. 4 in. (1.3 m.) long and a *tushker* (right), 4 ft. 2 in. (1.25 m.) long, found lying in the 'Tresta House' (see also Fig. 40).

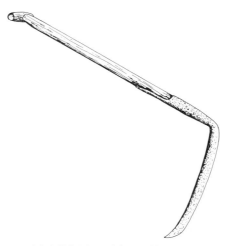

Fig. 38. A *ripper*, blade 15.5 in. (48.75 cm.) long. Made by an Orkney blacksmith, and now in the NMAS. Those used in Fetlar were similar, but as a rule had shorter blades.

moor spade resembled that of the delving spade, but was rounded instead of cut square across the face. This allowed it to cut when tilted at an angle, not just upright. When the slab of turf was clear, they would both jab their spades into it and sling it into the base or *greff* of the peat-bank. If another worker was at hand, or if the ground was wet, more care would be taken to lay the turves green side up, and fairly well placed to serve as a foundation for a row of peat (the *third peat*) put there to dry. The second way involved the ripper, and could readily be done by one man. The ripper was made by a smith, and consisted of a long blade, often made from an old rasp, socketed at an angle of 45°– 50° on to the end of a wooden shaft (Fig. 38). The blade was sharpened on the outer side, and the worker pushed it away from him as he worked along the top of the bank. Once the marking out was done, the spade was used to undercut the turves as before. This was a method much favoured on good quality banks, especially when there was rivalry between peat-casters to see who could make the best job. The ripper cut at an even depth and a smooth surface was left after the removal of the turf, making the tops of the peats level. Digging down with the top spade, on the other hand, made the tops of the peats uneven and untidy looking, and in plan gave a serrated appearance to the bank.

It often happened that with an extensive growth of heather or grass, even with the top turf removed there was still a depth of earthy moor, full of tough roots, not considered suitable for peat. In this case, a second layer had to be removed. This was known as *taking a poaning*. The resultant slabs were used for such jobs as building around stacks of peat left on the moor through the winter. Any wet oversized, and generally *taa-ey* (full of tough roots) peats cut during the cleaning of the bank, and usually wedge-shaped, were known as *skyumpacks*, *skyumpies* or sometimes *corner peats* since their shape made them useful in building up the corners of stacks at the house. They also served to even up sloping ground at the bank on which a row of peat was to be built to dry, and were used as fuel for cooking meals in the 'peat houses' on Lamb Hoga during the casting, raising, turning, and flitting of the peats.

The hardest work in peat-casting was cleaning *undermoors*. This was necessary when new banks were being opened on old peat moor that had already had two or three depths of peat removed, leaving more underneath. A great deal of clearing was needed to get down to the fresh peat, and for this a square garden spade was used. The process was called *skooming the bank*, and sometimes in the course of such work an old clay pipe or horn spoon, left by some earlier peat-caster, would come to light.

Once the surface turf had been removed, the underlying peat was ready to be cut by the *tushker* or peat-spade (Fig. 37, right). On Lamb Hoga, where the peat tended to be tough, a foot-peg or *heel* like that on the Shetland delving spade was added to the tushker, and the peats were *delled* (delved) out. On a good peat moor, no heel was needed, and the tushker was thrust in by the arms alone. This was called *running the peat*. When a lot of casting had to be done in a season, a leather palm with a thumb hole, like that used by saddlers, was often worn on the left hand to give protection.

The thickness of the peat was determined by the back of the tushker, and its width by the length of the feather. The average size of a peat was 14 inches long by 7 inches broad by 2½ inches thick, and the number in the width of the bank, known as the *ootburk* (or, in other parts of Shetland, the *shoard*), was generally seven or eight. The moor was usually three peats deep, more rarely four.

On the Mainland of Scotland, it was and is customary for one worker to cut the peat, and another to lift it off the spade and lay it out to dry. In Fetlar, and elsewhere in Shetland, both operations are performed by the caster. The first peats from the *first moor* were laid at the back of the bank, those from the next row down, the *second moor*, at the face of the bank, and those from the *third moor* at the bottom of the bank (the *greff*) on top of the surface turf and outer peats that served as a dry foundation or *steed* (Fig. 39). In good, well-drained banks, four moors were often cut, and two rows of peat built up in the greff. The first course usually consisted of tough peats, full of roots, and not easily broken. In Yell and many other parts of Shetland, these were laid out flat by the caster on the top of the bank in regular lines, one behind the other, space being left at the face for the second course to be built up in a *daek* (dyke). In Fetlar this method was not favoured since it was thought that the peats were better to be built up so that the weight squeezed out the water, producing a better-quality peat. Besides laying out, there were three methods of building peats — *kessed, stepped up*, and in *holed* dykes (Fig. 40). Kessed dykes were made up of vertical rows of peats, one immediately above the other, each row being known as a *kess*; holed dykes had narrow openings between the peats; and stepped up dykes were laid up like bricks, end over middle, with no air spaces. In every case the peats lay at a slight angle to the top of the

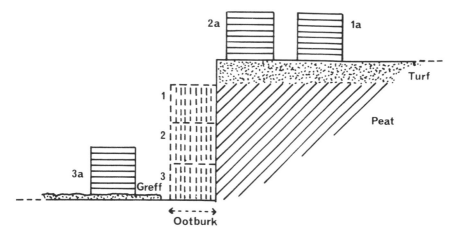

Fig. 39. Peat-casting diagram: 1. first moor, 1a. first peats, built at the *back* of the bank; 2. second moor, 2a. second peats, built at the *face* of the bank; 3. third moor, 3a. third peats, built in the *greff*. The *ootburk* is shown as eight peats wide. Dotted lines indicate the peat removed during peat casting.

bank as they came off the inverted blade of the tushker. The peats in the top row of the dyke were often set at an angle, side to shoulder, producing a zig-zag appearance. The making of a well-built dyke occasioned a good deal of rivalry. Holed and stepped dykes looked best, especially when finished off with a neatly angled row, but for practical reasons the kessed dyke was to be preferred, since during raising the whole kess could be carried or rolled out by the women folk, whereas the peats had to be handled individually in the other two forms.

Raising took place after the peats had been drying for two or three weeks. A good-sized peat, the *horse peat*, was set on its side, and four peats leaned on their ends against it, two at each side. Another, the *craa peat*, was laid on top at a sloping angle to run the water. In a further two or three weeks, two to four of the raisings were made into one.

Fig. 40. Methods of drying peat in Fetlar: left to right, a *kessed* dyke with 4 *kesses*; a *stepped-up* dyke; a *holed* dyke.

This was *turning the peats*, and was the final process before they were taken home, though if there were many wet peats that had not dried well on wet ground they would be *rooged* in small circular stacks, *roogs*, built round with turfy peats for protection, and left all winter.

The different kinds of peat were *taa-ey* peat, full of tough roots; mossy peat; *widdy* peat, found deep down and in some places like the mires of North Dale so full of large tough roots, apparently of trees, that they could not be cut with normal implements; black or blue peat, which was the best quality for burning and letting off heat for cooking. Small pieces of peat were known as *clods*. The wedge-shaped, turfy *skyumpies* or *corner peats* from the outer face of the bank were generally thrown in the greff, or up on the bank clear of the dykes for use in the ways described above.

Peat Flitting

The transporting or *flitting* of peats took place about July, and was carried on both by land and by sea. For carrying by land, a herd of ponies was maintained in Fetlar. Crofters could still be seen riding bareback on the little ponies, their feet dangling nearly to the ground, and at least one man used a pony yoked in a cart for leading in hay. The Fetlar ponies were particularly fine animals, said to be due to crossing with a grey Arab presented by General Bolivar to the then Sir Arthur Nicholson in 1837, and to a subsequent cross of another Arab and an Orkney garron (O'Dell 1939, 31, 83). Their main *raison d'être* was peat-carrying, and a good peat pony would soon learn the track it had to follow to get to a particular bank. There was generally one 'house-trained' pony that rounded up the others and kept them in line, and was ridden on the return journey to the hill by the peat-boy. Each household was expected to supply a peat-boy for leading the ponies back and forth during flitting. A round trip with a load or *led* of peats was a *geng*. Teams of a dozen to fourteen ponies loaded with peat might be driven in bunches, or travel in line with the halter of one tied to part of the harness of the one in front. This was known as *cringan* the ponies, and was the method employed on the longer journeys, such as to Funzie at the east side. They were then said to be in *crings*.

The peat was carried in straw baskets or *horse kishies* slung at the ponies' sides. The harness as a whole, including the baskets, was the *bend*, and when it was taken off, the pony was *aff-bendit*. First, a straw pad or *flackie* was laid on the pony's back. This was made of bunches

Fig. 41. Making a flackie in Fair Isle, *c.* 1920. Photograph lent by J. A. Mann.

Fig. 42. A peat pony with its *bend*, with the late Willie Park, Leagarth, his second wife Hannah (née Petrie), and his children Mary and Tom. Photograph lent by Mr and Mrs Jamieson, Beala.

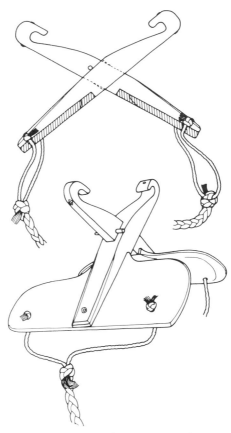

Fig. 43. A wooden saddle or *clibber* from Shetland, 16¼ in. (41.1 cm.) wide × 17¼ in.
(43.6 cm.) deep. In Fetlar, all *clibbers* noted had straight side-boards, without having
one side higher than the other.

of drawn-out straw or *gloy*, bound together side by side with binder
twine or handmade rope, *simmonts*, of bent grass or dried rushes (*floss*),
and sacking might be sown on to one or both sides to make it more
comfortable (Figs. 41-42). On to the flackie was set the wooden pack-
saddle or *clibber*. The Shetland saddles have a pair of horns, the *muckle*
and *peerie* —, or *she* and *he neevies* or *neebies*, placed centrally, and one
slotted through the other, with a wooden or iron pin, the *vernyaggle
pin*, hingeing them together (Fig. 43). In Orkney, on the other hand,
saddles usually have two pairs of horns, placed at the outer ends of the
side boards. A pair of holes in the lower side of each board took a rope,
the *gointick*, to which the belly-band or *wimegirt*, also of rope, was
attached. Finally, the *tailgirt*, which prevented loads from slipping

Fig. 44. Making a kishie.

forward, passed under the pony's tail, and was attached to the saddle. It had to be well padded to prevent grazing on the first day or two of flitting, but if this happened a linen bandage tied in a bow at the top, or a piece of chamois leather, was put round the sore part. If the saddle or flackie caused grazing, moss from the hill would be put in for extra padding. The *bend* was completed by a pair of straw *kishies*, and a pair of network bags or *maishies* of bent grass. The pony's bridle had a pair of wooden cheek-pieces. All of this harness could be easily made at home, although a crofter would sometimes specialise and make *kishies* in bulk which he sold to his neighbours. The late Willie Park, Leagarth, for example, made and sold *kishies* (cf. Fig. 44) for 1/6 each, the coir yarn for binding the straw (it would formerly have been *simmonts* of bent grass or dried rushes) being supplied to him. A great many *kishies* were required for peat flitting. A household flitting with ponies might have a team of 12-14, for which 24-28 kishies were required, and if, as sometimes happened, double sets were used so that one set could be ready filled at the bank pending the team's return, then 48-56 kishies had to be made. In terms of man-hours the making of such numbers of baskets, with flackies and maishies in addition, amounted to a considerable total and was one of the concealed ways in which the use of peat for fuel inhibited development, though the work was admittedly carried on during the winter evenings when not much else was possible. A horse kishie could be made in about three hours.

For making kishies, bands of drawn straw, as long as could be got, were laid out in twos, each pair together forming a straight line. The thin ends, from which the ears had been threshed, were made to overlap so that the double length of the band was of an even thickness throughout. In Fetlar the bands were called *hyogs*, derived from the Norse word for *eye*, and in some parts of Shetland the scotticised term *een* (eyes) was used. The bands were doubled over and the first turn of the coir yarn or simmont that bound them together was made along the line of the doubling, and formed the bottom of the kishie which was then built up with successive turns till the top was reached (Fig. 44). In order to give the sides their necessary rounding and extension, extra hyogs were set in, forming a triangular panel at each side. The loose ends of these added hyogs were trimmed off where they protruded inside the kishie. The rim was made by doubling back the ends of the hyogs and binding round the double thickness. This was the only part of the work where an implement of any kind was required, a needle of wood or bone, about 8 inches long, with a ½ inch diameter hole at the thick end. With it, the simmont was pulled through, taken round two hyogs, pulled tight, passed back between these, taken round two again, and so on. Once the rim was bound, the kishie was finished except for trimming off or *stooing* the loose ends of the hyogs, and fixing a *carring* (carrying) *band* to the *bearing band*, which is usually the third band or *geng* of simmonts down from the rim (Fig. 45).

The smaller kishie used on horses was the horse kishie; the one carried on people's backs when loading peat boats was bigger, and had a carrying band at each side. A type also used on horseback, but not so common, was the *reppa-kishie*, simply an openwork kishie made of dried rushes and coir yarn in the same manner as a *maishie* (see below), but less rigid.

In binding the hyogs of the kishie tightly together, it was necessary to pull one end of the simmont with the hand, whilst gripping the other in the teeth. This could only be done as long as the maker had teeth, and the particular tooth used to grip the band was jocularly referred to as the *kishie-makin' yackle*. It was, however, possible to overcome the difficulty by fixing a wooden hook to a board that could be strapped across the chest (Fig. 46). Alternatively, an iron hook served with heavy twine, and fastened to a belt, might be used.

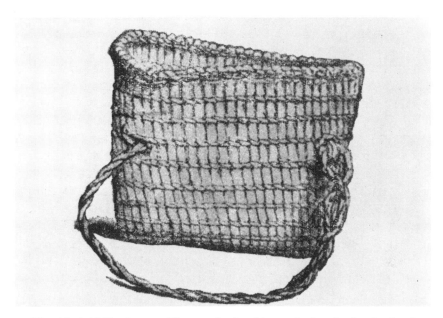

Fig. 45. A *kishie* of straw. The *carrying band* is attached to the *bearing band*.

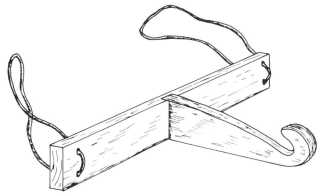

Fig. 46. A wooden hook used in kishie-making by Robert John Jamieson, Beala, now in the National Museum. Base 8 × 1½ in. (20 × 3.75 cm.); hook, 5 in. (12.5 cm.) long.

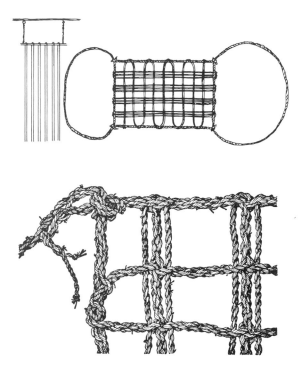

Fig. 47. Making a *maishie*. Top: 1. *simmonts* over a stick slung from the ceiling (left); 2. the completed *maishie* with shorter *under fettle* and longer *upper fettle* (right); 3. detail of corner showing methods of linking the parts.

The making of maishies (Fig. 47) was said to be the most interesting job in building up a set of peat-flitting equipment. They took the form of rectangular nets, about 3 ft. × 2 ft., and were of straw, dried rushes, bent grass or coir yarn. Maishies made entirely of rushes were very good, but in Mr Laurenson's opinion, the ideal was a combination of coir yarn and rushes. Bundles of rushes made up for maishie-making were as big as could be squeezed into the *yarkin'* of the hand, i.e., the outstretched thumb and forefinger.

Maishies were made to two patterns. The first had longitudinal bands in groups of three, the centre band in each group being double, and each group being about a hand's breadth apart. The second was made so as to have equal-sized meshes or *eyes*, and was rather more common. The earliest known illustration of a maishie, dating from 1770 in Orkney (where the name is *maisie*), is of the latter form. This is inset on 'A Chart of the Orkney Islands, in which are printed out the Lands of the Earldom belonging to the Right Honourable Sr Laurence

Dundas, Baronet', by William Aberdeen, *c.* 1770 (now in Kirkwall Public Library).

Where coir yarn and rushes were being used, the longitudinal bands were of rushes and the cross bands and surrounding band of coir yarn, which was laid two ply on a rope-twister (*tuimikins*) (Fenton III (1961), 154). In finishing off the border, a third strand of coir yarn, called the *aboot-gaan-störie*, was added by hand.

The work was begun by suspending a stick with a cord at each end from the kitchen roof (Fig. 47). Simmonts of double length, four to six in number, were hung over it at equal distances apart. The first eyes were made by twisting five turns with the thumb and forefinger into the top of each double simmont, and then dipping the ends through the twin strands of the first cross band of coir yarn, the halves of the simmont going one at each side of a twist in the cross band to give strength and to keep it in place (Fig. 47). The work proceeded on this pattern, always counting say five turns down and five across to keep the eyes equal, until the maishie was filled in. After this the outer border was put on, a wooden spike being used to open the eyes, through which it had to go in the ends of the cross bands. The stick was withdrawn at the top, and the border band passed through the loops that were left. At the bottom the spare ends were tucked back, and the aboot-gan-störie, wound into the border by hand, gripped the loops and tucked-back ends in place. The border was drawn out at each corner to form a lug to which the ends of the carrying bands, the upper and under *fettle*, were attached. The under fettle was the shorter of the two, and when it was looped round the far side of the saddle, the end of the maishie should reach the ground. The upper fettle was made longer for adjustment, and was fastened round the horn of the saddle. During peat flitting it was doubled and shortened, but for carrying sheaves it was kept full length.

Peat flitting began at about 2 o'clock in the morning and went on till midday. Five to seven *leds* (loads), each involving a double journey, could be carried in one spell of work. Normally the women piled up the peat at the bank and filled the kishies ready for transport. They were the *uplayers* (Fig. 48). When the kishie had been partly filled it could be stacked round the edge with big *taa-ey* peats to extend the rim, and the extra space filled with loose clods of peat. The fettle of the maishie was unhooked and laid on the ground, the kishie was set into the maishie, then the fettle was brought back up and hooked on to the horn of the saddle again so that the peats would form an even, rounded

Fig. 48. Four *uplayers*, Tommy Garriock, Hendry Jameson, Magnie and Bobby Bruce, filling horse *kishies*. Photograph lent by T. Garriock, Funzie.

load at the pony's side. The loads were generally turned, that is, the kishies were set on to the open maishie in such a way that when the fettle was brought up, the kishie turned upside down. Loads that were turned could be well topped up. They might also be *set up*, so that the kishies lay upright in the maishie. This was the method used with young or aged mares, and the peats were not heaped much for fear of falling off. Two people were required, one at each side of the mare, to put on the load, and if they were turning a load they would tell each other the number and quality of peats they had stowed in, saying, for example, 'Thirty widdy, — blue, — taa-ey, — mossy". This helped in judging the balance of the load, a very necessary thing on the steep, uneven tracks. The kishies themselves were carefully matched for size in pairs, and often a piece of coloured string was tied into the lips of a matching pair. Latterly, peats were carried in sacks, so it mattered less if a load fell off. The big, turfy skyumpies were often carried in the maishie without a kishie at all.

When a lot of mares were coming and going at the same time along the peat roads it was sometimes difficult to prevent a mix-up between loaded and unloaded ones. The most difficult part was when flitting to the boats in the Geo of Lamb Hoga (Moowick) in thick fog. Light mares had to give way to loaded mares. At one spot above the Geo, the people coming down with a loaded mare had to shout or whistle. On hearing this, the people in the Geo had to decide if they could get up in time so as to avoid running into them. The same applied when flitting home in narrow parts of the peat road at the Klevie of Tresta and the Klifts.

In earlier times when there were enough people for each household to do its own peat-flitting, practically all the peats were *flit* by boats, both sixareens with three pairs of oars, and fourareens, with two pairs of oars. As the population dropped, the amount of flitting by boat decreased, flitting by pony increased and several families started working together. It is only in the early 1900s that flitting home with ponies came into fashion in the townships of Tresta and Hubie.

There were ten loading places for peat on Lamb Hoga (Fig. 36): Inner Daal, Da Rousker, Ooter Daal, Geo of Lamb Hoga or Moowick, Seli Geo, Da Horn, Sinni-berg, Mailand, Lambhellia-cuddies, Skersoond. Of these, leaving aside the Geo of Moowick, Mailand was the shortest and easiest for loading, Seli Geo the most difficult and dangerous.

The peats were flit to these places, and built in stacks on the ground above the landing places. They had to be carried on the back down to the boat in big peat kishies. These had an extra carrying band, and a man going up with an empty kishie would meet his fellow at the halfway mark, give him the empty one, and turn round and take the full one on to his back. This halved the amount of climbing involved. The loaders spread out evenly over the distance from stack to boat so as to work in pairs as described. At the stack there were people to fill the kishies, and at the boat there was a *lifter on* who passed up the peats, from where they were emptied, to the fillers in the boat. The skipper built up the peats at each end of the boat. The last kishies were set in without being emptied, and the extra hands sat on them, as did members of the crew (which might comprise both men and women) when the boat was under sail and rowing was not necessary. The peats were well built at the aft end to prevent people or kishies from falling off. To Mr Laurenson's knowledge, the only person to be drowned during flitting by boat was a young woman who was sitting aft and fell off the kishies when the boat struck a rock at Lamb Hoga Head. One boat, the *Margaret*, a Funzie fourareen, ran under a tide lump at Snap Point and nearly foundered. The *Charlotte*, a Beala fourareen, had a

narrow escape coming from Seli Geo in a rough sea, through being
overloaded.

The Geo of Moowick was probably the most important of the peat
loading places (Fig. 49), but differed from the others in being a beach.
Accordingly, special loading facilities had to be provided for the boats.
They were termed *noosts*, a Norse term normally applied to boat
shelters above high water mark. Shingle was shovelled out to form a
dock, and both sides were built up with large flat stones. They have all
been filled in, but their outlines are still visible at low water. The east
one was known as the Noost of Smithfield, having been made for
Gilbert Smith who had nine sixareens for flitting peat for his mansion
house (built in 1815) of Smithfield. The west noost was made by Irvine
Park of Beala, one of the greatest of the Fetlar sixareen skippers
(Laurenson 63 (1962), 22) and his sons. The noosts were prepared
immediately before the peat flitting by their users who would go with
shovels, picks, etc., in small boats. A day in the noosts was a hard one,
and much sweat was lost, since the winter storms and heavy seas did
much damage and filled them with stones and shingle.

At the home beaches the boat came alongside a wooden *tress* or
jetty, and the flitters had a meal of tea, bread and butter, etc., before
offloading, using the same methods, but in reverse, as for loading.
Each family had its own space for its *roog* or stack on the beach, and
the stacks had to be flitted home from there on the backs of ponies, or
in carts by those who had them. Finally, the big stacks containing the
whole of the peat harvest were built at home. They were rectangular in
shape, with rounded corners made with wedge-shaped skyumpies, and
drawn in towards the top, which was often thatched with flat slabs of
turf (*poans* or *feals*). Some workers built round the outside, where the
peats had to be set carefully, and others filled up the centre. A ladder
or *peat trap* was required for the higher stages.

It will thus be seen that flitting by pony involved much less handling
of the peat than flitting by boat. With ponies, the full kishies had one
journey. With boats, they had two journeys on the backs of the mares,
and two more on the backs of the loaders. This extra effort, requiring
greater manpower, was undoubtedly responsible for flitting by boat
being given up earlier than flitting by pony as the population declined.
Boats finally went out of use in the 1940s, and the last flitter to use
ponies was Tommy Thomason, of Vailzie, about 1956.

Fig. 49. Peat flitting by boat from Moowick. From a watercolour by T. Train, *c.* 1930.

Peat Houses

When casting was in progress the men usually travelled from their homes to Lamb Hoga and back each day, but during peat flitting the workers, both male and female, lived in temporary quarters on the banks, known as *peat hooses*. To some extent these represent a degree of modernisation, since they are said to have been built only about 1860. Before that, the only form of shelter was an old sail spread over the peat flitters.

The list of peat houses and their owners is as follows:

1. The Barn. An old croft house, consisting of house, barn, and byre (Figs. 50-51). The middle part was used as a peat-house by the late William Garriock of Funzie, and the east part by the late William Laurence Brown of Funzie.
2. John Mouat's House, at the South Tolgans. Roofed, and could have been made habitable. Its owner, John Mouat of Hubie, died 23 January 1964.

3. Robert John Jamieson's house at the Lower Tolgans. Its owner lived at Beala.

4. William Park's house, Mid Tolgans.

5. The Nort' Hoose o' Tolgans, owned by the late Andrew Brown of Funzie.

6. Crü o' Helliersness. A croft house until 1830. Jointly owned by Laurence Robertson, Henry Anderson and Laurence Bain, all of Tresta, and all deceased.

7. Lower Hoose of Helliersness, owned by the late Daniel Brown.

8. East Hoose of Helliersness, owned by the late Robert Scollay of Tresta.

9. Mid Hoose, in Helliersness, owned by the late Thomas Peterson of Tresta.

10. Nort' Hoose, in Helliersness, built for the West Manse minister, the late Rev. Jas. A. Campbell, who hired people to flit his peats.

11. Tresta Hoose, in Helliersness, jointly owned by Davie Anderson, North Dale and John Robertson, Tansy Knowes.

12. Nort' Hoose, Gilles Field, jointly owned by James Petrie and William Gardner, both deceased.

13. Hoose o' Heoga Neep, owned by the late James Coutts of Hubie.

A small number of these still survived with walls and to a lesser extent roofs intact. These are the Tresta House and Crü, both at Helliersness, John Mouat's house at South Tolgans, and the Barn at Moowick. The remainder are represented by the foundations of walls that had been built of turf. The majority were sunk into the side of a peat bank so that the lower course of the walls was of solid peat. These smaller houses always had the fire in the corner opposite the door, as in the Nort' Hoose, Gilles Field (Fig. 52). The fireplace was made of large stones set at right angles to provide a back and base, and care had to be taken that the dry turf walls were covered sufficiently to prevent them catching fire. The bigger houses, on the other hand, had fireplaces in the centre of a gable wall, and one had a hearth and chimney recessed into the wall (Figs. 53, 50).

In the Barn, with its stone gable, and in John Mouat's house, with its turf gable, the fireplace was built out into the room, and had massive stone sides whose tops formed level platforms on which things could be laid (Figs. 51, 54, 50). The chimneys took the form of three-sided wooden canopies nailed to the rafters and pinned against the wall.

Fig. 50. The Barn. The roof is thatched with turf. The initials on the wooden *happer* (chimney) are those of Willie Thomason. There is a cupboard in each of the corners. Dimensions: 49 ft. (14.7 m.) long × 15 ft. (4.5 m.) wide.

Fig. 51. Interior of the Barn, *c.* 1920-30.

Fig. 52. The hearth of the Nort' House, Gilles Field.

Fig. 53. The Tresta House, Helliersness.

Fig. 54. The hearth in John Mouat's house.

These were called *happers* (hoppers) since they resembled in shape the hopper of a mill (Fig. 55). In the Barn, the happer was originally topped by a half barrel. The smaller houses had chimneys built of turf, which could be altered by being built up higher on the windward side to provide a better draught. This process was called to *skyle da lum*, an expression elsewhere applied to altering the draught by means of a wooden board. An iron bar, the *cross-baak*, driven into the stonework of the chimney or laid across two stones, served to support the crook and links, or more often a twisted piece of fencing wire, on which the kettle and pot was hung above the fire. There were benches along the walls, a table and such crockery as was required. The feature common to all the houses was the plank-covered bed-space, occupying at least half the area of the floor (Figs. 56, 50, 55). The planks were supported above the floor on posts, or else a wall or *burbank* of turf was built about two feet high at each side, and the planks laid across. The space below served as a store for spare maishies, clibbers, boots, etc. On the first journey out to Lamb Hoga, when flitting was about to start, straw was carried in bags and spread on the planks of the bed. Heather could also be used. Then a cover of sacking was laid over the straw, followed by a sheet, made from two sewn together. The blankets were also sewn together in pairs, and similarly for the patchwork quilt that completed

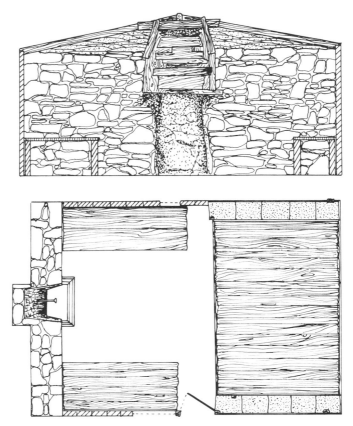

Fig. 55. The Tresta House, Helliersness. The stone gable has been built out at the back to allow recessing of the chimney. Dimensions: 17 ft. 2 in. (5.15 m.) long by 11 ft. 10 in. (3.55 m.) wide.

the bed. The group of workers based on each house slept here indiscriminately.

Just as the form of the canopy-type chimney carried on the now almost obsolete 'wid (wood) - funnel' tradition of ordinary dwelling houses in Fetlar and elsewhere in Shetland, so also did the form of the door (Fig. 57). The latch was of wood, and could be opened by a length of string fastened to it by a nail, and brought through a small hole in the door, so that the string could be pulled and the door opened from outside. The hinges were of wood. The upright parts on the jamb of the door were the *charl-pins*. The cross bars on the door were the *harrs*. The upper ends of the charl-pins were shaped into round pins, and holes were bored into the thicker end of the harrs, to fit on to these pins. Leather washers were used to minimise wear.

Fig. 56. Tresta House interior, showing the bed space. II.7.4A.

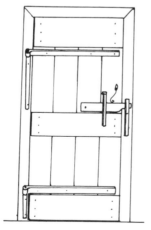

Fig. 57. The door of the Tresta House, with its wooden sneck. Dimensions: 4 ft. 6 in. (1.35 m.) high × 2 ft. (60 cm.) wide.

The walls of the Barn and the Crü of Helliersness were entirely of stone, except for turf gable tops; the Tresta Hoose had a stone gable and walls partly of wood, partly of turf; John Mouat's house was of turf. The roofs were simply made of a ridge-pole and six to nine pairs of couples. *Ovey-boards* or laths overlay the couples, and the thatch on top of this was of turf. When the houses were being slept in, an old sail was tied over the roof above the bed-space to keep off the drips. The Tresta House and John Mouat's house were modernised with corrugated iron. There was a smaller window, *peerie glig*, in one corner in the roof of the Barn, but no trace of this remains. The turf houses were sometimes roofed simply with a sail laid over a rigging tree, and pegged down at the sides.

Life in the peat houses was clearly enjoyed by all, and many stories of boyish pranks are told. One of the worst was to upset the pony harness when the people were in bed, and mix up maishies, flackies, and kishies together. Milk set outside in bottles in a cold moor hole to keep it from going sour would be drunk by any young fellows finding it. Doors were tied up so that people could not get out, and chimneys blocked to smoke them a little. Any good-looking girls were always sure of visitors, and had to put up with them whether they wanted to or not.

Food supplies were easy enough for those who were flitting home with ponies, but those who were flitting to the loading places for the boats stayed on Lamb Hoga for a week. A bag of meal and a grid-iron were necessities for them as was the *piltock wand*, a long rod without a reel for catching young coalfish. There were numerous *craig* seats in the rocks around Lamb Hoga where fishing went on. Potatoes and hard fish were also taken. Sometimes a little borrowing went on in an indirect way, with the conversation going: 'I might have to affbend da mares and geng hame fur breid?' 'Na lamb, du needna do dat, we can gi'e dee what'll keep dee gaan ta Saturday, only we wid like a boil o' fresh piltocks if du can faa (spare) dat sam'.

When the last of the peats had been loaded, and the party was ready to return, the straw or heather was cleared off the planks in the bed space and piled up outside. More heather was plucked until the heap was a good size, and then it was set alight. The bonfire was something greatly looked forward to by the youngsters, and the smoke told the people in the townships that the flitting season was over and the flitters would soon be home.

Appendix

Mr Laurenson has also contributed stories and items of historical interest that form a background to the practical aspects of peat flitting from Lamb Hoga. These are as follows:

1. There were formerly five inhabited crofts in Lamb Hoga — two at Helliersness, one at Mailand, one at Moowick, one at Burgastoon. The remains of some are still visible on the ground, and their head dykes can be picked up on air photographs. Four fell vacant about 1830 as a result of evictions by the proprietor, Sir Arthur Nicholson, and eventually came to be used as peat houses. The Moowick croft was a good one, and was occupied by William Brown, who moved to Oddsetter. Burgastoon was deserted much earlier as it was believed to be haunted. Its stones have been used for building a dyke at a dangerous cliff nearby to keep stock from falling over. It was situated near to and bearing north-east from Ramsness, and was the most secluded of the Lamb Hoga crofts. Some time about the year 1680, a tragedy that was never explained took place here. The men of the five crofts formed the crew of a sixareen and on the day of the story they had been at Urie in the north of Fetlar with their fish. On their return they drew the boat up on the beach at Moowick, and the crew proceeded to their homes. The man of Burgastoon was alarmed to note, when still a distance from his house, that everything looked strangely quiet, and no smoke was issuing from the chimney. His fears grew as he drew nearer, for neither his wife nor his two children were about to welcome him as usual. He found the doors left open and his family lying dead on the floor in a welter of blood, wounded about the head and face.

The officials of the island went to investigate, but the only potential clue they found was a wooden-soled clog, dry in the inside, floating in at the rocks at the shore nearby. It was said that a strange-looking sailing ship was seen south of Fetlar about that time, so it was generally assumed that men from her had landed and murdered the crofter's family. The truth, however, was never clearly known. It is said that the place became haunted and that animals grazing there cleared out when the sun went down.

There is very little green grass about Burgastoon now in comparison with what there is around other crofts, since it fell vacant so much earlier.

2. In July 1840, a crofter in Setter, Laurence Petrie, took four halters and a büdie (fish basket made of docken stalks) full of grass,

and went to the hill with his seven-year-old son, Gilbert, to catch his four mares to begin peat-flitting in Lamb Hoga. He found two at the Loch of Heogapund, enticed them with the grass and led them to a *plantie-crub* (enclosure for growing kail from seed) at Halyra-Kirk nearby, and told the boy to stop there with the mares while he went further away to look for the other two. To make sure the boy kept a hold of them, he tied each *halter-shank* (head-rope) to one of his wrists.

After a long search he found the other mares and returned to the plantie crub, but no trace of his son and the two mares was to be seen. He assumed that he would find the boy at home and did not worry. On reaching home, however, his wife told him there was no sign of their son. Alarmed, he had a quick meal, got two of his neighbours and set out to search. They found the boy near the Loch of Heogapund, dead. For some reason the mares had bolted, dragging the boy by the wrists, until, passing one at each side of a large stone, the mares were brought to a standstill by their human anchor.

To this day, Fetlar children are specially warned about getting twists and turns of the head-rope around their wrists and hands, in case any similar tragedy should occur.

3. Anyone walking over the ground in Lamb Hoga between South Tolgans and the new dyke that runs from Moowick over Gilles Field to the Klifts will see bare patches of ground and occasionally of black ash. These mark the site of the great fire of Lamb Hoga, 55 years ago.

The loss in peats was, fortunately, slight, since most folk who had peats in the area of the fire had already transported them to the loading places. One man who was later in starting flitting, however, dropped a fragment of a lighted peat when carrying it in a tongs from another peat house to kindle a fire in his own. He did not look round and did not see that the heather was alight. It was only when the flitters got up in the morning that they saw the extent of the fire, and realised it had too firm a hold for anything to be done. The local press headlined the 'Great Fire in Fetlar', which kept burning till subdued by the rain and snow of winter. Though the Laird made enquiries about how it started, no one could tell.

Acknowledgements

Amongst the many people in Fetlar who helped on various topics during my stay there, thanks are due for information on peat-flitting to

Kenneth and Mimie Hughson, Leagarth, John Mouat, Hubie, George Williamson and Tommy Garriock, both at Funzie, Davie Anderson, North Dale, John Robertson, Tansy Knowes, Willie Petrie, Aith Ness and the Jamieson family at Beala. My greatest debt is to the late James Laurenson, Aithbank, who willingly made available his immense knowledge of Fetlar when I was on the island, and subsequently read through this essay in draft form and greatly improved and expanded it.

References

Abd. Jnl. Aberdeen Journal

Act. Dom. Conc. Acts of the Lords of Council in Civil Causes

Adam, R. J., ed. *John Home's Survey of Assynt* (Scottish History Society) Edinburgh 1960

Agricultural Mag. The Agricultural Magazine IX (1811)

Aiton, W. (a) *General View of the Agriculture of the County of Ayr* Glasgow 1811

Aiton, W. (b) *A Treatise on the Origin, Qualities, and Cultivation of Moss-Earth* Ayr 1811

Alexander, W. *Northern Rural Life in the Eighteenth Century* Edinburgh 1877

Allan, J. Agriculture in Aberdeenshire in the Sixties. In *The Deeside Field* 1927

Anderson, J. *General View of the Agriculture of the County of Aberdeen* Edinburgh 1794

Anon. 1750 *An Exact and Authentic Account of the . . . White-Herring Fishery in Scotland* London 1750

Anon. III Ian Mitchell, A., ed. *Geographical Collections relating to Scotland made by Walter Macfarlane* (Scottish History Society) Edinburgh 1907

AP Acts of Parliament

Arbroath T. C. Minutes Arbroath Town Council Minutes, 1727-40 (Manuscript)

Arbuthnot, J. A True Method of treating Light Hazely Ground . . . containing Rules for Infields, Outfields, Haughs and Laighs (Edinburgh 1735). In Souter, D. *General View of the Agriculture of Banff* Edinburgh 1812, Appendix, 83-8

Bailey, J. and Culley, G. *General View of the Agriculture of Northumberland* London 1794

Bro-Jorgensen, M. Billeder af Viborg amts Forhistorie. In *Historisk Samfund for Viborg amt* 1966, 116-18

Barron, D. G., ed. *The Court Book of the Barony of Urie* (Scottish History Society) Edinburgh 1892

Barry, G. *The History of the Orkney Islands* Edinburgh 1805

Bath, Slicher van *The Agrarian History of Western Europe, A.D. 500-1850* London 1963

Belsches, R. *General View of the Agriculture of Stirling* Edinburgh 1796

Ben, Jo. Descriptio Insularum Orchediarum. In Macfarlane, W., ed. *Geographical Collections relating to Scotland* (Scottish History Society) Edinburgh 1908

Beveridge, E. *North Uist, its Archaeology and Topography* Edinburgh 1911

Black Illustrated catalogue of Goods Manufactured by Thomas Black & Sons, Limited Sea View Works, Berwick-on-Tweed (no date)

Brand, J. *A Brief Description of Orkney, Zetland, Pightland Firth and Caithness* (1683) Edinburgh 1701

Brereton, Sir W. Travels. In Brown, P. H. *Early Travellers in Scotland* Edinburgh 1891

Brown, P. H. *Early Travellers in Scotland* Edinburgh 1891

Buchan-Hepburn, A. G. *General View of the Agriculture of East Lothian* Edinburgh 1794

Burnett, G., ed. *Exchequer Rolls of Scotland*, IV quoted in *DOST* 1880

Burnett, J. H., ed. *The Vegetation of Scotland* Edinburgh, London 1964

Caird, J. *English Agriculture* London 1852

Caled. Mag. Caledonian Magazine

Caledonian Mercury Quoted in SND s.v. *Muirburn*

Campbell, J. *Political Survey of Britain* London 1774

Carmichael, A. *Carmina Gadelica. Ortha nan Gaidheal* Edinburgh, London 1928-1971

Carruthers, W. Garve to the Lews. In *Transactions of the Inverness Scientific Society and Field Club* 1875-80

Catalogue 1841 Catalogue of the Museum of the Highland and Agricultural Society Edinburgh 1841

Catalogue 1892 Catalogue of the National Museum of Antiquities of Scotland Edinburgh 1892, 348: 'MP219, yoke of wood, 41½ in. long, from moss near Lochnell, Argyllshire — Hubert Paton 1890.'

Christison, D. Carvings and Inscriptions on the Kirkyard Monuments of the Scottish Lowlands. In *Proceedings of the Society of Antiquaries of Scotland* 36 (1901-2); 39 (1904-5)

Collections Collections for a History of the Shires of Aberdeen and Banff (Spalding Club) Aberdeen 1843

Cowie, R. *Shetland and its Inhabitants* (1871) Lerwick 1879

Cramond, W. *The Annals of Banff* (New Spalding Club) Aberdeen 1891

Cramond, W. *The Church of Aberdour* Fraserburgh 1896

Cregeen, E. ed. *Argyll Estate Instructions* (Scottish History Society) Edinburgh 1964

Darling, F. Fraser *Crofting Agriculture. Its Practice in the West Highlands and Islands* Edinburgh, London 1945

Darling, F. Fraser *West Highland Survey* Oxford 1955

Delamarre, Jean-Brunhes. *Géographie et ethnologie de l'attelage au joug en France du XVIIe siècle à nos jours* Uherské Hradiště 1969

Dickinson, C. I. *British Seaweeds* London 1963

Dickson, A. *Treatise of Agriculture* Edinburgh 1770

Dickson, R. W. *Practical Agriculture* London 1805

Djurhuus, N. ed. Svabo, J. C. *Indberetninger fra en Reise i Faeroe 1781 og*

1782 København 1959

Dodgshon, R. A. and Jewell, C. A. Paring and Burning and Related Practices with particular reference to the South-Western Counties of England. In Gailey, A. and Fenton, A., (eds.) *The Spade in Northern and Atlantic Europe* Belfast 1970, 76-87

Donaldson, J. E. *Caithness in the 18th Century* Edinburgh, London 1938

Donaldson, G. *The Court Book of Shetland* (Scottish Record Society) Edinburgh 1954

DOST Dictionary of the Older Scottish Tongue

Douglas, R. *General View of the Agriculture of Roxburgh and Selkirk* 1813

Drack, W. Wagengräber und Wagenbestandteile aus Hallstattgrabhügeln der Schweiz. In *Zeitschrift für Schweizerische Archäologie und Kunstgeschichte* V, 18 (1958), 12-17

Driver, A. & W. *General View of the Agriculture of Hampshire* 1794

Dunbar, E. D. *Social Life in Former Days* Edinburgh 1865

Dwelly, E. *The Illustrated Gaelic–English Dictionary* Glasgow 1949

Edmondston, A. *A View of the Ancient and Present State of the Zetland Islands* Edinburgh 1809

Erixon, S. *Atlas över svensk Folkkultur* (Part I) Uddevalla 1957

Evans, E. E. *Irish Folk Ways* London 1957

Extracts Extracts from the Records of the Burgh of Peebles (Scottish Burgh Records Society) 1910

Farrall, T. On the Agriculture of the Islands of Orkney. In *Transactions of the Highland and Agricultural Society of Scotland* VI (1874)

Fea Diary Manuscript Diary of Patrick Fea. Transcript in National Museum

Fenton, A. Ropes and Rope-making in Scotland. In *Gwerin* III (1961), 142-56, 200-14

Fenton, A. Early and Traditional Cultivating Implements in Scotland. In *Proceedings of the Society of Antiquaries of Scotland* 96 (1962-3), 264-317

Fenton, A. Draught Oxen in Britain. In Jacobeit, W. and Kramařik, J., eds. *Rinderanschirrung* (Národopísný Věstník Československý) III-IV (1968-69)

Fenton, A. Transport with Pack Horse and Slide-Car in Scotland. In Fenton, A., Podolak, J. and Rasmussen, R. (eds.) *Land Transport in Europe* Copenhagen 1973

Fenton, A. *The Northern Isles: Orkney and Shetland* Edinburgh 1978

Fenton, A. Early Manuring Techniques. In Mercer, R., ed. *Farming Practice in British Prehistory* Edinburgh 1981, 210-17

Filip, J. *Celtic Civilisation and its Heritage* Prague 1962

Firth, J. *Reminiscences of an Orkney Parish* (1920) Stromness 1974

Foord, Wm. & Rbt. MS James' Account Book, 1806-15. In National Museum of Antiquities of Scotland

Forbes III The Forbes Baron Court Book. In *Miscellany of the Scottish History Society* (Scottish History Society) Edinburgh 1919

Forsyth, R. *Beauties of Scotland* Edinburgh 1805-8

Fox, C. Sleds, Carts and Wagons. In *Antiquity* V (1931), 185-99

Fullerton, J. *Records of the Burgh of Prestwick, 1470-1782* (Maitland Club) Glasgow 1834

Fussell, G. E. The Breast Plough. In *Man* 33 (1933), 109-14

Fussell, G. E. Four Centuries of Farming Systems in Sussex, 1500-1900. In *Sussex Archaeological Collections* XC (1952), 60-101

Gandert, O.-F. Zur Frage der Rinderanschirrung im Neolithikum. In *Jahrbuch des Römisch-Germanischen Zentralmuseums Mainz* V, II (1964), 37-38

Gifford, T. *A Historical Description of the Zetland Islands* (1786) London 1879

Gordon of Straloch, R. In Mitchell, A., ed. *Geographical Collections relating to Scotland made by Walter Macfarlane* (Scottish History Society) Edinburgh 1907

Graham, P. *General View of the Agriculture of Stirling* Edinburgh 1812

Graham, P. *General View of the Agriculture of Kinross* Edinburgh 1814

Gregor, MSS. Quoted in *The Scottish National Dictionary*

Gregor, W. *The Folk-lore of the North East of Scotland* London 1881

Gregor, W. Some old Farming Customs and Notions in Aberdeenshire. In *Folk-Lore Journal* II (1884)

Hagar, H. Marknadsok. In *Folk-Liv* (1952), 5-17

Hagar, H. Bidrag till dragoxhandelns historia i Sverige. In *Folk-Liv* XXX (1966), 23-31

Hamilton, H. *Selections from the Monymusk Estate Papers* (1713-55) (Scottish History Society) Edinburgh 1945

Hamilton, H. *Life and Labour on an Aberdeenshire Estate, 1735-50* (Third Spalding Club) Aberdeen 1946

Haudricourt, A. and Delamarre, M. J. B. *L'Homme et la Charrue à Travers le Monde* Paris 1955

Havinden, M. A. *Household and Farm Inventories in Oxfordshire, 1550-1590* (Historical Manuscripts Commission) London 1965

Hayen, H. Das Doppeljoch aus dem Petersfehner Moor. In *Archäologische Mitteilungen aus Nordwestdeutschland* 6 (1983), 12-22

Headrick, J. *View of the Mineralogy, Agriculture, Manufactures and Fisheries of the Island of Arran* Edinburgh 1807

Headrick, J. *General View of the Agriculture of Angus* Edinburgh 1813

Henderson, J. *General View of the Agriculture of Caithness* London 1812

Henderson, J. *General View of the Agriculture of Sutherland* London 1812

Hennell, T. *Change in the Farm* Cambridge 1934

Hewat, K. *A Little Scottish World* Kilmarnock 1894

Hibbert, S. *A Description of the Shetland Islands* Edinburgh 1822

Holm Holm Forge Company, Bellshill, Catalogue, Spades and Shovels (no date)

Home, J. *Rectified Report of Berwickshire Agriculture* Berwick 1794

Jackson, J. *Treatise on Agriculture and Dairy Husbandry* 1850

Jackson, P. Scottish Seaweed Resources. In *Scottish Geographical Magazine* 64/3 (1948)

Jacobeit, W. Ein eisenzeitliches Joch aus Nordirland. In *Ethnographische-Archäologische Forschungen* I (1953), 95-7

Jacobeit, W. and Kramařík, J. (eds.), *Rinderanschirrung* (Národopisný Věstník Československý) III-IV (1968-1969)

Jenkins, J. G. *Agricultural Transport in Wales* Cardiff 1962

Johnston, A. W. and Johnston, A. *Diplomatarium Orcadense et Hialtlandense* London 1907-13

Johnston, B. *General View of the Agriculture of Dumfries* London 1794

Johnston, J. *Terra Lindisfarnensis; the Natural History of the Eastern Borders* London 1853

Johnston, T. *General View of the Agriculture of Selkirk* London 1794

Kames, Lord (Henry Home) *The Gentleman Farmer* Edinburgh 1776

Keith, G. S. *General View of the Agriculture of Aberdeenshire* Aberdeen 1811

Kenyon, G. H. The Civil Defence and Livestock Returns for Sussex in 1801. In *Sussex Archaeological Collections* LXXXIX (1950), 57-84

Kerr, R. *General View of the Agriculture of Berwick* London 1809

Killip, I. M. The Work of the Manx Ploughman. In *Journal of the Manx Museum* VII (1966), 2-5

Laurenson, J. J. Da Sixern Days. In *The New Shetlander* No. 63 (1962)

Leask, J. T. S. Dividing Sea-Weed 100 years ago. In *Orkney and Shetland Miscellany*. *Old-Lore Series* I (1907-8), 33-4

Leask, J. T. S. Shipping Peats from Orkney. In *Ib*. I (1907-8), 129-34

Legge, W. H. Glimpses of Ancient Agriculture. In *The Reliquary* XI (1905)

Lerche, G. Die nach der Radiokarbonmethode altersbestimmten dänischen Pfluggeräte. In *Tools and Tillage* I:1 (1968), 58-60

Leslie, W. *General View of the Agriculture of Nairn and Moray* London 1811

Liber Liber S Thome de Aberbrothoc (Bannatyne Club) I (1848); II (1856)

Low, D. *Elements of Practical Agriculture* Edinburgh 1834

Low, G. *A Tour through the Islands of Orkney and Schetland* Kirkwall 1879

Lowe, R. *General View of the Agriculture of Nottingham* London 1794

Macdonald, A. Some Rare Gaelic Words and Phrases. In *Transactions of the Gaelic Society of Inverness* 29 (1915)

Macdonald, D. Some Rare Words and Phrases. In *Transactions of the Gaelic Society of Inverness* XXXVII (1934)

McDonald, Rev. Fr. A. *Gaelic Words and Expressions from South Uist and Eriskay* (ed. J. L. Campbell) Dublin 1958

Macdonald, J. *General View of the Agriculture of the Hebrides* Edinburgh 1811

Macfarlane, W. *Genealogical Collections Concerning Families in Scotland* (Scottish History Society) Edinburgh 1900

Macfarlane, W. *Geographical Collections Relating to Scotland* (Scottish History Society) Edinburgh 1906-8

Mackaile, M. A Short Relation of the Most Considerable Things in Orkney. In Macfarlane, W., *op. cit.*, III, 1-7

Mackay, R. J. *Old Days in a Highland Fishing Village* Aberdeen n.d.

McKeller Manuscript Joiner's Account Book. In private possession

Mackenzie, G. S. *A General Survey of the Counties of Ross and Sutherland* London 1810

Mackenzie, O. H. *A Hundred Years in the Highlands* London 1949

Mackintosh, W. of Borlum. *An Essay on Ways and Means for Inclosing, Fallowing, Planting &c Scotland* Edinburgh 1729

Mackie, J. Manuscript Diary. In private possession

Mair, G. *Narratives and Extracts from the Records of the Presbytery of Ellon* Peterhead 1894

Marshall, W. *The Rural Economy of the Southern Counties* London 1798

Martin, M. *A Description of the Western Isles of Scotland* (1703) Glasgow 1884

Marwick, H. *A Dictionary of the Orkney Norn* Oxford 1929

Marwick, H. Two Orkney 18th Century Inventories. In *Proceedings of the Orkney Antiquarian Society* XII (1934), 47-54

Marwick, H. *Merchant Lairds of Long Ago* Kirkwall 1939

Megaw, B.R.S. Farming and Fishing Scenes on a Caithness Plan. In *Scottish Studies* VI (1962), 218-23

MERL Museum of English Rural Life

Misc. N.S.C. Miscellany of the New Spalding Club Aberdeen 1908

Moisley, H. A. *Uig. A Hebridean Parish* Glasgow, Nottingham 1962

Mortimer, J. *The Whole Art of Husbandry* (1707) London 1708

Munro, R. W. *Munro's Western Isles of Scotland and Genealogies of the Clans 1549* Edinburgh, London 1961

Murray, J. E. L. The Agriculture of Crail, 1550-1600. In *Scottish Studies* 8/1 (1964), 85-95

Naismith, J. *General View of the Agriculture of Clydesdale* Glasgow 1798

Naismith, J. On Manures . . . In Sinclair, Sir J. *Appendix to The General Report of the Agricultural State and Political Circumstances of Scotland* Edinburgh, 1814

Nielsen, H. G. *Læsøfolk i Gamle Dage* (people of Læsø in olden days) (Danmarks Folkeminder Nr. 29) København 1924

NMAS National Museum of Antiquities of Scotland

NSA New (Second) Statistical Account

Ochterlony, J. Account of the Shire of Forfar. In *The Spottiswoode Miscellany* Edinburgh 1844

O'Dell, A. *The Historical Geography of the Shetland Islands* Lerwick 1939

Old Lore Misc. Old Lore Miscellany

Omond, J. *Orkney 80 years ago* Kirkwall 1911

O'Neill, T. Some Irish Techniques of Gathering Seaweed. In *Folk Life* 8 (1970), 13-19

Oral Information. From A. Hutcheon, Crathes; L. Jaffray, Insch; A. Anderson, Stonehaven; J. Ironside, Aberdeen

OSA Old (First) Statistical Account

Owen, A. *Ancient Laws and Institutes of Wales* I, London 1841

Pálsson, H. & Edwards, P. *Orkneyinga Saga. The History of the Earls of Orkney* London 1978

Payne, F. G. The Plough in Ancient Britain. In *The Archaeological Journal* CIV (1948), 82-111

Payne, F. G. *Yr Aradr Gymreig* Cardiff 1954

Peat Surveys Scottish Peat Surveys (Department of Agriculture and Fisheries for Scotland) I-IV (1964)

Pennant, T. *A Tour in Scotland MDCCLXIX* London 1776

Peterkin, A. *Rentals of the Ancient Earldom and Bishoprick of Orkney* Edinburgh 1820

Private Acts Acts 12 & 13 Victoria (Private) London 1849

Piggott, S. An Iron Age Yoke from Northern Ireland. In *Proceedings of the Prehistoric Society* XV (1949), 192-3

Piggott, S. *Ancient Europe* Edinburgh 1965

Piggott, S. The Earliest Wheeled Vehicles and the Caucasian Evidence. In *Proceedings of the Prehistoric Society* XXXIV (1969)

Pococke, R. *Tours in Scotland, 1747, 1750, 1760* (Scottish History Society) Edinburgh 1887

Pratt, J. B. *Buchan* (1858) Aberdeen 1870

Quayle, B. *General View of the Agriculture of the Isle of Man* London 1794

Quayle, T. *General View of the Agriculture of the Isle of Man* London 1812

Reg. Mag. Sig. Scot. The Register of the Great Seal of Scotland

Reg. P. C. Scot. Register of the Privy Council of Scotland

Rennie, R. On Paring and Burning. In Sinclair, Sir J. *General Report of the Agricultural State of Scotland* Edinburgh 1814, II, 403-18

Report 1878 Report on the Present State of the Agriculture of Scotland Edinburgh 1878

Report 1884 Report of Her Majesty's Commissioners of Inquiry into the Condition of the Crofters and Cottars in the Highlands and Islands of Scotland Edinburgh 1884

Richards, M. *The Laws of Hywel Dda* Liverpool 1954

Richardson, H. G. The Medieval Plough-Team. In *History* XXVI (1942)

Rigg Illustrated Catalogue of Solid Steel Spades and Shovels, Hill Drain and Tile Drain Tools, manufactured by James Rigg and Sons, Crawick Forge, Sanquhar, Dumfries-shire, Scotland (no date)

Robertson, G. *General View of the Agriculture of Kincardineshire or, The Mearns* London 1813

Robertson, J. *General View of the Agriculture in the Southern Districts of Perth* London 1794

Robertson, J. *General View of the Agriculture of Perth* Perth 1799

Robertson, J. *General View of the Agriculture in the County of Inverness* London 1808

Rogers, C. Register of the Collegiate Church of Crail. In *Transactions of the Royal Historical Society* VI (1877)

Rothes MSS. In Kirkcaldy Museum

Salzman, L. F. The Property of the Earl of Arundel, 1397. In *Sussex Archaeological Collections* XCI (1953), 32-52

Sandison, S. *Unst: my island home and its story* Lerwick 1968

Schmidt, L. Der randbeschlagene Holzspaten in Ostmitteleuropa. In *Deutsches Jahrbuch für Volkskunde* 3 (1957)

Scott Catalogue of T. Scott & Co., Ltd., Wholesale Ironmongers, 47-51 Grassmarket, Edinburgh (List No. 61) (no date)

Scott, M. A. *Island Saga. The Story of North Ronaldsay* Aberdeen 1968

Seebohm, M. E. *Evolution of the English Farm* London 1927

Session Papers Session Papers, Earl of Morton v. Covingtree (Signet Library 46, 21)

Shaw, M. F. *Folksongs and Folklore of South Uist* London 1955

Shirreff, J. *General View of the Agriculture of the Orkney Islands* Edinburgh 1814

Shirreff, J. *General View of the Agriculture of the Shetland Islands* Edinburgh 1814

Simpson, E. J. Farm Carts and Wagons of the Orkney Islands. In *Scottish Studies* VII/2 (1963), 154-69

Sinclair, J. *Survey of the Agriculture of the Northern Counties* London 1795

Sinclair, J. *General Report of the Agricultural State, and Political Circumstances of Scotland* London 1814

Sinclair, J. On the Improvement of Mossy Lands. In Steele A. *A History of Peat Moss* Edinburgh 1826

Singer, Dr *General View of the Agriculture of Dumfries* Edinburgh 1812

Skinner, B. C. *The Cramond Iron Works* (Edinburgh University Department of Adult Education and Extra-Mural Studies) Edinburgh 1965

Skirving, R. S. On the Agriculture of the Islands of Shetland. In *Transactions of the Highland and Agricultural Society of Scotland* VI (1874), 229-64

Smith, D. On the Propriety of Burning Heath Ground, for the Improvement of Pasture. In *Prize Essays and Transactions of the Highland Society* I (1799)

Smith, J. *General View of the Agriculture of the County of Argyll* Edinburgh 1798

Smith, J. H. *The Gordon's Mill Farming Club, 1758-64* Aberdeen 1962

Smith, S. *General View of the Agriculture of Galloway* London 1810

Smith, W. Dividing Seaweed in Sandwick, Orkney. In *Orkney and Shetland Miscellany. Old-Lore Series* V (1912)

SND Scottish National Dictionary

Somerville, R. *General View of the Agriculture of East Lothian* London 1805

Souter, D. *General View of the Agriculture of Banff* Edinburgh 1812

Steele, A. *A History of Peat Moss* Edinburgh 1826

Steensberg, A. North West European Plough Types. In *Acta Archaeologica* VII (1936), 244-80

Stephens, H. *The Book of the Farm* Edinburgh, London 1844

Tait Manuscript Diaries 1890-1922. In private possession

Taylor, A. B. *The Orkneyinga Saga* Edinburgh, London 1938

Thirsk, J., ed. *The Agrarian History of England and Wales (IV, 1500-1640)* Cambridge 1967

Thomson, J. *General View of the Agriculture of Fife* Edinburgh 1800

Transactions Transactions of the Society for the Encouragement of Arts, Manufactures and Commerce II (1789), 81

Trans. Roy. Hist. Soc. Transactions of the Royal Historical Society

Turner, E. The Marchant Diary. In *Sussex Archaeological Collections* XXV (1873), 163-99

Uhlig, H. Old Hamlets with Infield and Outfield Systems. In *Geografiska Annaler* 43 (1961)

UJA Ulster Journal of Archaeology

Ure, A. *General View of the Agriculture of Dumbarton* London 1794

Vilkuna, K. Die Verwendung von Zugochsen in Finnland. In *Studia Fennica* II (1936)

Walker, D. Essay on Peat. In *Prize Essays of the Highland Society* 2 (1803)

Walker, J. *An Economical History of the Hebrides and Highlands of Scotland* London 1812

Wallace, J. *A Description of the Isles of Orkney* (1700) Edinburgh 1883

White, L. *Medieval Technology and Social Change* Oxford 1964

Whyte, A. and Macfarlan, D. *General View of the Agriculture of Dumbarton* Glasgow 1811

Wight, A. *Present State of Husbandry in Scotland* Edinburgh 1778-1784

Wilson, A. E. Farming in Sussex in the Middle Ages. In *Sussex Archaeological Collections* XCVII (1959), 98-118

Wilson, J. *General View of the Agriculture of Renfrewshire* Paisley 1812

Wolfe George Wolfe and Sons Ltd., Bathgate, Scotland, Spade and Shovel Catalogue (no date)

Wood, J. P. *The Ancient and Modern State of the Parish of Cramond* 1794

Young, A. *General View of the Agriculture of the County of Sussex* London 1793

Young, A. *General View of the Agriculture of the County of Sussex* London 1808

Other Books of Interest

The Shape of the Past, Volume 1, by Alexander Fenton, ISBN 0 85976 129 0, 200 pages, 45 illustrations, £12.00

CONTENTS Material Culture in Local History Studies. Historical Ethnology. An Approach to Folk Life Studies. Regional Ethnology and Environmental Awareness. The Scope of Regional Ethnology. Aspects of the North-East Personality. Change and Conservatism in the Farm Villages of Lewis. The Longhouse in Northern Scotland. A Fuel of Necessity: Animal Manure. Sickle, Scythe and Reaping Machine: a Study in Innovation Patterns. Hand Threshing.

The first five chapters outline a working theoretical approach to folk life studies that has been largely evolved from first principles and the remaining six contain examples of the resulting practice. Information has been assembled from printed and oral sources, from museums and private collections, from dialect and dictionaries, and from archaeology. The analysis of this accumulated detail makes a substantive contribution to European ethnology.

'Alexander Fenton writes with the precision of the man who knows his facts and the caution of the man who knows the limitations of his knowledge. The limitations of anyone's knowledge. He is not quite like the banished Duke in *As You Like It*, finding 'sermons in stones', but only because he doesn't preach at the reader. Instead he finds history in the stones, and in so doing, opens up for us a new window on Scotland's past.' *Stornoway Gazette*

Scottish Country Life, by Alexander Fenton, ISBN 0 85976 011 1, 266 pages, 120 illustrations, £7.00

CONTENTS The Face of the Land. Tilling the Soil. Harvesting the Grain. Threshing the Grain. Drying and Grinding the Grain. Root Crops. The Shieling. Milk, Butter and Cheese. Everyday Food. Farm and Steading. Fuel for the Fire. Transport. The Farming Community. Conclusion.

'This must be the definitive work on the subject. The vast and varied field of agricultural practice during the centuries and over all Scotland is his subject, and he writes engagingly with unobtrusive scholarship of its every aspect — farming practice, implements, drains, dykes, crafts, fairs and markets, food and drink. At a time when mechanisation and standardisation is the rule, this book is more than ever valuable, and must become a standard source for future generations to study and enjoy.' *National Trust Newsletter* 'This book is a veritable treasurehouse of factual material appertaining to country life as it has been lived through the centuries, not only in the Scottish lowlands but also in the Highlands and Islands.' *Scots Magazine*

The Northern Isles, by Alexander Fenton, ISBN 0 85976 019 7, 732 pages, 287 illustrations, £18.00

CONTENTS The Shape of Things. Farm and Township: Pattern of Settlement. Homes and Working Places. Fuel for the Fire. Back Transport, Harness and Straw Working. Baskets and Ropes. The Land and its Produce. Draught Animals and Transport. Cereal Crops. Root Crops and Gardening. Cattle and Milk Products. Sheep and Textiles. Pigs, Rabbits and Geese. The Shore and the Sea.

'It is a part of Mr Fenton's stupendous achievement that beyond exploring in vivid detail how the islanders conducted their lives in the past, he has clearly demonstrated how their unique culture evolved over a long period. Excellent illustrations, supporting the verbal description, an extensive bibliography and an invaluable index, all combine to make this publication a most remarkable event.' *Northern Studies* 'It is a delight and privilege to welcome a book by Alexander Fenton which recreates the physical environment in which the people lived, the work with crops and beasts, the harvest of the sea, the houses, the food they ate. It is a massive piece of scholarship, an encyclopaedia of the material culture of Orkney and Shetland, and will assuredly become the classic work of reference in this field for many years to come. An indispensable work for anyone interested in the traditional life of Orkney and Shetland.' *New Shetlander*

Review of Scottish Culture 1, edited by Alexander Fenton with Hugh Cheape and Rosalind K. Marshall, ISBN 0 85976 106 1, 112 pages, 30 illustrations, £5.00

CONTENTS The Wreck of the Lastdrager. Wooden Tumbler Locks

in Scotland and Beyond. Lewis Shielings. The Clay Tobacco Pipe Collection in the National Museum. Wet-Nursing in Scotland, 1500-1800. Tenements: a Pre-Industrial Urban Tradition. Box Beds and Bannocks: The Living Past. Scottish Agricultural Improvement Societies. A Scottish Historical Atlas. A Mill and Kiln at Kirtomy, Sutherland.

The aim of ROSC is to provide an annual review of the material aspects of Scottish social and economic history, covering rural and urban, maritime and land-based topics, the applied and decorative arts and the actions and interactions and conditions of the people. '*Review of Scottish Culture* should lack neither readers or well-informed contributions judging by the quality of the contents of this first issue.' *History Teaching Review*

'Written, edited, illustrated and published to a very high standard, we are rarely presented with so much fascinating information in one compact volume at this price.' *Scottish Local History*

Review of Scottish Culture 2, edited by Alexander Fenton with Hugh Cheape and Rosalind K. Marshall, ISBN 0 85976 138 X, 120 pages, 30 illustrations, £5.00

CONTENTS The Wearing of Wedding Rings in Scotland. The Book Designs of Talwin Morris, 1865-1911. 'Plaister Gimcracks': the Handicraft of Allan Ramsay the Poet. The Plague in the Grass: Grass Sickness in Horses. William Marshall, Agricultural Writer in Scotland. Notes on Long Line Fishing from Arbroath, Ferryden and Gordoun. Who Were the Sailormen? Food on Sunday. Destruction, Damage and Decay: The Collapse of Scottish Medieval Buildings. Tenements: the Industrial Legacy. An Early Sixteenth Century French Architectural Source for the Palace of Falkland. A Project in Experimental Archaeology: Avasjo, 1982. Post-Medieval Pots and Potters at Throsk in Stirlingshire. Dr I. F. Grant, 1887-1983: The Highland Folk Museum and a Bibliography of her Written Works.

Food in Perspective: Third International Conference of Ethnological Food Research, edited by Alexander Fenton and Trefor M. Owen, ISBN 0 85976 044 8, 440 pages 60 illustrations, £20.00

CONTENTS The World Food Crisis, Ethnological Food Research,

and Museums. A Preference Food: The Philadelphia Soft Pretzel. The Thrive-Bit — A Study of Cultural Adaptation. Bread in Ireland. Some Symbolic Aspects of Food Products in the Light of a Thirteenth Century Polish Historical Source. The Social Functions of Festival Food: A Few Thoughts on an Investigation in Northern Sweden. The Privileged Position of Farinaceous Foods in Austria. The Cookery Book as a Document for Cultural and Social History. Frozen Dinners — the Staple Emergency: Meals of a Changing Modern Society. Food and Meals in a Congested District: County Donegal in 1891. The Significance of Food in Religious Ideology and Behaviour in Marathi Myths. Plants and Weeds as a Food of the People: An Example from West Steiermark, Austria. Freshly Consumed Flat Bread in the near East. Ethnological Characteristics of Traditional Wheat Flour Foods in Bulgaria. The Diffusion Channels of Urban Food Habits. Starting an Anthropology Handbook on Food Habits for the Knowledge of Man's Food Behaviour. The Diet of Women in Childbirth. The Preference for Sweets, Spices and Almond Milk in Late Medieval English Cuisine. The Making of Health Wine in the Fifteenth Century in Hungary, and the Role of Wine in the Diet and Medicine of the People at the Present Day. The Social Aspects of the Diet of the Polish People, with Special Reference to Preferences and Taboos. The Potato in Finnish Food Economy. The Beginnings of the Modern Milk Age in Germany. Greek Immigrant Cuisine in America: Continuity and Change. On the Origins and Development of Preferences and Taboos in Eating and Drinking. The Impact of the Introduction of Maize into the Food of the Rumanian People. The First Ethnic Cook Book in the United States. An Interdependence of Foodways and Architecture: A Foodways Context on the American Plains. Food and Traditional Verbal Modes in the Social Control of Children. Food in a Medical System: Prescriptions and Proscriptions in Health and Illness among Malays. The Use of Cannabis in two Cookery Books of the Fifteenth Century. The Sausage Culture of the Pennsylvania Germans.

'This is a substantial dish full of historical nourishment, economic, social and agrarian and nicely peppered with quantitative seasoning.' *Irish Economic and Social History* 'A most valuable contribution to the knowledge of all nations.' *Lore and Language*

Food in Change: Eating Habits from the Middle Ages to the Present Day, edited by Alexander Fenton and Eszter Kisbán, ISBN 0 85976 145 2, 224 pages, 4 illustrations, £15.00

CONTENTS Diet and Social Movements in the U.S.A. Philadelphia Bread Reassessed. Pottery and Food Preparation, Storage and Transport in the Scottish Hebrides. Fasting and Working Monks, 5th-11th Century Regulations. Food and the Coastal Environment. Hard Tack as Popular Food. Food Habits in Change, The Example of Europe. Change in the Polish Farmers' Kitchen after the Potato. Changes in Country Eating Habits in West Steiermark after the Second World War. Integration Processes in the Popular Diet of the South Moravian Border Region. Continuity and Change in Irish Diet. Turning Points in the History of Popular Diet in Slovakia. Major Periods of Change in the Food of Russian Towns in the 16th-19th Centuries. Periods and Turning Points in the History of Bulgarian Food. Results of Ethnocartographic Research into the Popular Food of Slovakia. Bourgeois Influences on Polish Food and Diet, Directions and Periods of Change. Periods and Gaps in the History of Food in Europe, an Outline of Problems and Methods. Popular Rumanian food at the Turn of the 18th-19th Century. White Gravies in American Popular Diet. Potato Spirits in Early Days. Obligatory Fasts and Voluntary Asceticism in the Middle Ages.

Based on contributions to the Fourth International Conference of Ethnological Food Research this book shows how diet and eating habits have changed over the centuries.

The Northern and Western Isles in the Viking World, edited by Alexander Fenton and Hermann Pálsson, ISBN 0 85976 101 0, 300 pages, 60 illustrations, £20.00

CONTENTS Graves and Grave Goods: Survey and Evaluation. The Norse Buildings at Skaill, Deerness, Orkney and their Immediate Predecessor. Papa Stour: Survival, Continuity and Change in One Shetland Island. Soapstone Quarrying in Viking Lands. Boats and Boatbuilding in Western Norway and the Islands. Building Traditions in the Northern World. Fishermen and Boats. Northern Links: Continuity and Change. Viking Settlements in the Northern and Western Isles: the Place-name Evidence as seen from Denmark and the Danelaw. Settlement, Society and Church Organisation in the Northern Isles. Icelandic-Scottish Contacts: Sir William Craigie, Séra Einar Gudmundsson and *Skotlands Rímor*. Recounting Traditions: A Critical View of Medieval Reportage. Runes. Arnórr Pórdarson: Skald of the Orkney Jarls. A Florilegium in Norse from Medieval Orkney. The

Vikings in Gaelic Oral Tradition. A Critical Review of the Work of Jakob Jakobsen and Hugh Marwick. Faroese Folktale Tradition. A Sense of Place: An Exercise in Interpretation and Communication.

'What can one say of such a book as this or who can criticise the leading European experts when writing on their specific fields of knowledge? I found it a fascinating book, well written and produced with good clear type and of a size which handled nicely, and full of good explanatory drawings, maps, reconstructions and illustrations and in my opinion, well worth its cost.' *New Shetlander*

Loads and Roads in Scotland and Beyond, edited by Alexander Fenton and Geoffrey Stell, ISBN 0 85976 107 X, 160 pages, 62 illustrations, £8.50

CONTENTS Prehistoric Roads and Trackways in Britain — Problems and Possibilities. The Evidence From The Roman Period. Land Routes — The Medieval Evidence. Bridges and Roads in Scotland, 1400-1750. Old Bridge, Bridge of Earn — a Posthumous Account. Wheelless Transport in Northern Scotland. The Distribution of Carts and Wagons.

'The collection is well illustrated and annotated and makes a very stimulating and significant addition to our shelves, because it presents clearly and with great authority the sort of information and ideas which we need.' *Scottish Local History* 'The importance of this collection to students of archaeology and ancient and medieval history is obvious; yet there is plenty to attract and hold the attention of the non-specialist.' *Books in Scotland*

The Rural Architecture of Scotland, by Alexander Fenton and Bruce Walker, ISBN 0 85976 020 0, 256 pages, 195 illustrations, £15.00

CONTENTS The Care of Buildings. Survey Bodies and Archives. Printed Sources. Surveys and Survey Methods. Roofing Materials. Walling Materials. The Layout of Farm Buildings, with Their Furniture and Fittings, 1750-1850. The Housing of Farm Workers. The Influence of Technology on Farm Buildings. A Sample Survey: Grampian Region. Conclusion.

'It has achieved a multi-disciplinary approach to its subject through the contrasting expertise of its two authors. This combination of skills is of especial importance in the study of farm architecture where a knowledge of the form of agricultural buildings is meaningless without an appreciation of their function. As an introduction to the present state of knowledge it succeeds admirably in its purpose. Future architectural and agricultural historians of Scotland will need to draw extensively upon this work.' *Museums Journal* 'This is a book of great significance, well illustrated with superb photographs.' *Times Literary Supplement*

The Making of the Crofting Community, by James Hunter, ISBN 0 85976 014 6, 350 pages, £12.00

CONTENTS Introduction. The End of an Old Order: The Highlands in the 18th Century. The Beginnings of Crofting, 1800-1820. A Redundant Population, 1821-1844. Famine, 1845-1850. Fewer People, Less Land, 1850-1857. The Emergence of the Crofting Community. The Years of Recovery: Crofting Society, 1858-1880. The Highland Land War 1: Beginnings, 1881-1883. The Highland Land War 2: Is Treasa Tuath na Tighearna, 1884-1886. The Highland Land War 3: Coercion and Conciliation, 1886-1896. Land Raids and Land Settlement, 1897-1930. Postscript: The Crofting Community Today.

'Dr Hunter has written this history with controlled passion and savage exactness. He has presented the facts duly referenced and there is an invaluable bibliography. This book should be in every library.' *Glasgow Herald*

The Scottish Antiquarian Tradition, edited by A. S. Bell, ISBN 0 85976 080 4, 296 pages, 10 illustrations, £15.00

CONTENTS David Steuart Erskine, 11th Earl of Buchan: Founder of the Society of Antiquaries of Scotland. The Museum, its Beginnings and its Development. 'A Fine, Genial, Hearty Band': David Laing, Daniel Wilson, and Scottish Archaeology. Scottish Archaeology in the Second Half of the Nineteenth Century. The National Museum to 1954. In Piam Veterum Memoriam. Two Centuries of Scottish Numismatics. The Arms of the Society of Antiquaries of Scotland. The Society's Charter: A Translation. Lists of the Presidents of the Society, and of Keepers and Directors of the National Museum of Antiquities.

'A sparkling collection of essays, reflecting light on more than the obscurer recesses of the Society of Antiquaries of Scotland. It throws light on the early development of archaeology in Great Britain and it shows that while much may change, people and the problems they cause, don't. This book should be on every archaeologist's, historian's and sociologist's bookshelf.' *Popular Archaeology*

Studies in Scottish Antiquity, edited by David J. Breeze, ISBN 0 85976 075 8, 480 pages, 206 illustrations, £30.00

CONTENTS Introduction. SHC. Callanish. The Roman Fort on the Antonine Wall at Bearsden. The Northern Frontier of the Anglo-Saxons. Major Early Monasteries. Norman Settlement in Galloway. Mediaeval Wooden Bowls. Scottish Mediaeval Window Tracery. Documents concerning the King's Works at Linlithgow 1302-3. Scottish Renaissance Architecture. The De Wet Paintings in the Chapel at Glamis Castle. Lauderdale at Holyrood House, 1669-70. Towards a Study of Scottish Gardening from the 16th Century to the 18th. John Cheere and the Duke of Atholl. Scottish Parliamentary Churches and Manses. The Office of Works in Scotland: the Early Years. Victorian Mews in Edinburgh. The Architecture of McGibbon and Ross. Overton: Three Generations of a West Lothian Farm. The Defences of the Firth of Forth. Thirty Years of Popular Archaeology, 1945-1975. Bibliography of Works of Stewart Cruden.

'This *Festschrift*, in honour of Stewart Cruden, is for once both attractive to the well-rounded reader and worthy of the well-rounded scholar it honours. Whether British archaeology, in the broad sense, strikes you as young and fresh, old and clapped-out, or just a little middle-aged, it's nice to see a regular injection of timeless learning.' *Encounter*

Index

179